Your Super Powers!

JOSEPH MURPHY'S GOLDEN LESSONS

Your Super Powers!

A Master Class in Using the Magic Within

by Joseph Murphy

Author of *The Power of Your Subconscious Mind*

Edited by
Mitch Horowitz

MEDIA

Published 2021 by Gildan Media LLC
aka G&D Media
www.GandDmedia.com

Front cover design by David Rheinhardt of Pyrographx

Interior design by Meghan Day Healey of Story Horse, LLC

Library of Congress Cataloging-in-Publication Data is available
upon request

ISBN 978-1-7225-0556-1

10 9 8 7 6 5 4 3 2 1

CONTENTS

PREFACE:
"WE HAVE FORGOTTEN WHO WE ARE"

"We have forgotten who we are,
and we are trying to remember."

This how Joseph Murphy frames humanity's predicament in the essay that opens this collection.

Murphy dedicated his long career to awakening readers and listeners from their slumber—from their forgetfulness that, as beings fashioned in the image of Infinite Mind or whatever term one uses for the force of creativity, they, too, are beings capable of creation, causation, and even world-making.

Murphy saw life as a master class in the experience of realizing, or recalling, yourself as a creative being. He saw death not as an end but an enteral return to the source of Higher Mind from which all things emerge.

In this collection, Murphy refers to humanity as possessing greater powers—call them super powers—waiting to be refined, honed, and used, so that the individual can knowingly shape his or her world, rather than be shaped by chronic, rambling, and runaway thoughts. The seat of all power, Murphy taught, is emotionalized thought itself. All skills, abilities, and attainments are products of that greatest of powers.

•   •   •

We all live by assumptions. This is true whether we call ourselves believers, agnostics, materialists, or any other range of descriptions for how we relate to surrounding forces. Murphy challenges you to live by the *assumption of greatness*—of your relation to, and ability to wield, the esoteric powers of thought. If you accept his premise, and if you test it and find it promising, that act will go a long way toward engendering the feeling state that Murphy identifies as the royal road to harnessing and using your thoughts as tools of creation. "Feeling is the secret," wrote Murphy's friend and contemporary Neville Goddard. I am certain that Murphy would have agreed in every way with that statement. Combining thought and feeling, he taught, is the gateway to realizing your super nature: your power to create.

•   •   •

One of the points Murphy makes in this collection— especially in his essay "Realize Your Desire"—is that *desire itself is sacred*. Desire and need are goads to performance, ingenuity, and change. Without desire we would stagnate. We would suffer sameness and moribundity. We are conditioned to define desire as a longing; an unfulfilled desire can be painful. But Murphy's encouragement is to *greet desire as a hunger that delivers you.* A hunger that pushes you to know yourself. If you follow his vision, you will discover yourself as a being of vaster dimensions than you imagined.

Desire, need, hunger—do you feel these things right now? You must if you picked up this book. Good. Those are the impulses that summon you to your super-self. To your realization that desire exists not to punctuate your sense of lack but to point you toward its fulfillment. Read this collection in a state of desire. And see if that desire, combined with the keys you find here, does not help you recall the being that you truly are.

—*Mitch Horowitz*

Your 12 Powers

This book is about the 12 powers within you. Sometimes they're referred to as the 12 signs of the zodiac, the 12 sons of Jacob, the 12 months of the year, the 12 hours in the day, the 12 powers of Hercules, the 12 tribes of Israel, the 12 gates of heavenly Jerusalem, the 12 pillars of the temple of Heliopolis, the 12 stars of Janus, the 12 shields of Mars, the 12 mansions of the moon, and the 12 apostles symbolized and portrayed. The 12 powers of man are the elements of consciousness.

The zodiac means the holy belt of animals within you. In other words, infinity, or the 12 powers. These powers must be disciplined and purified before you become illumined, before you become the God-man walking the earth.

The 12 sons of Jacob represent the 12 disciples also. Their names and meanings are referred to in Genesis as Reuben, Simeon, Levi, and so on. In Matthew they're called Andrew, Peter, James, and John. They mean the same thing. It is our mission and purpose in life to discipline these faculties so that a Godlike man will appear on earth. Then like Job we can say, "*Yet in my flesh shall I see God.*"

Job asked this question as well, "*Where wast thou when I laid the foundation of the earth? Declare if thou hast understanding. Whereupon are the foundations that are fastened, who had laid the cornerstone thereof, when the morning stars sang together, and the sons of God shouted for joy?*" This is not a question asked of God by Job, but it is really a question asked by man of his higher self.

We have forgotten who we are, and we are trying to remember. Original sin has nothing to do with the physical sex act. It is man believing in the wisdom of the world, of the opinions of man, and using his intellect destructively.

Original sin simply means that man has forgotten his divine origin and accepts the opinions of men as the truth. Consequently, he errs because he does not know that his own I Am-ness is the Lord God Almighty. He dwells therefore in the land of many gods and the belief in many powers.

The man who loves truth and practices the presence of God is like a magnetized piece of steel. The man who is asleep to God is like a demagnetized piece of steel. The magnetic current is there, but it is asleep within him.

When we dwell in the presence of God, the electronic and atomic structure of our body reforms and vibrates accordingly. *"Canst thou bring forth Mazzaroth in his season, or canst though guide Arcturus with his sons?"* When you look up the concordance for the word Mazzaroth, you find it's the 12 powers of the zodiac, which are within yourself.

If we call our disciples forth and fully discipline them by prayer, by meditation and mystic visioning, we can answer all these questions propounded in that 38th chapter of Job. When man is completely purified consciously and subconsciously, the distillate brought forth is the illumined mind, called the God consciousness or cosmic consciousness.

Let each one determine for himself if he's calling forth these faculties. Andrew, called Reuben in Genesis, means "to behold the son." The son means the presence of God in you. Andrew is perception, perceiving the presence of God within you, or the truth of being. Andrew therefore means spiritual perception as the first faculty of man. Spiritual seeing means understanding, illumination, and comprehension, just like when you understand the answer to an algebraic equation. You say, "I see."

This is not three-dimensional seeing, but seeing the truth about the outer fact. If you put a stick in a pond or a lake or a river, it seems to be bent. But it isn't, it's an optical illusion. For example if you see two tracks in a railroad they seem to come together at the horizon. They don't; they're parallel. That would be seeing the truth about things.

The spiritual person sees the law of cause and effect operating everywhere, and he knows there is a subjective pattern behind all manifestation in his body and affairs. He knows the realization of his desire is the truth that sets him free. When you begin to see spiritually, you see peace where discord is, love where hatred is, joy where sadness is, light where darkness is, and life where so-called death is.

You see the presence of God where confusion is. We look at the atmosphere, and we say that there is nothing there, yet it is teeming with life. We look into the heavens and we see some stars, but when we look through a telescope we see many more stars not discerned by the naked eye. Which is right, the telescope or the eye? Many think the sun rises in the east and sets in the west, but spiritual seeing or understanding knows this is untrue.

If someone is sick in your family, how do you see them? If you see them unwell, you're not disciplining Andrew. Your spiritual perception, or knowing, must be perfect vision of health and happiness. If your mother is sick, see her home. She's happy, joyous, and free, bubbling over with enthusiasm. You're seeing the truth about her.

Do you resist, resent, or fight conditions in your home or office? If you do, you're not calling Andrew to discipleship. If you detach yourself from the problem and focus on the solution or the way out, realizing an Almighty power is backing you up, you're on the way to mastering this power.

* * *

All these faculties are within you, remember, and the zodiac is within you. The 12 sons of Jacob are within you, the 12 disciples. Peter is the second disciple, or faculty of the mind. He symbolizes the rock of truth, an immutable conviction of good. Peter is the faculty of mind that realizes God indwells him and walks and talks in him.

Peter is the type of mind that knows that the *I Am* within you is God, and there is no other God. Peter is faithful to the end. That is, you're faithful every step of the way, knowing omnipotence is moving on your behalf and, *"That none can stay His hand and say unto Him, what doest thou?"*

Do you say to the ideal or desire murmuring in your heart, "I am too old, I do not have enough money, I do not know the right people?" Do you say, for example,

that due to conditions, inflation, the present adminis-
tration, events, or circumstances, "It is impossible for
me to realize my objective?"

If this is so, you're not disciplining Peter, but actually robbing yourself of the joy of experiencing your
ideal. The faculty of faith called Peter knows no obstacles and recognizes no master or Lord except his own
I Am-ness, *"For I am the Lord. That is my name. My glory
you shall not give to another. Neither shall you give my
praise."*

Do you pray for a little while, then give up and say,
"I tried it, but it doesn't work?" If you do, you must
begin now to call Peter to discipleship, and you will
realize the cherished desire of your heart. Peter is faith
every step of the way, faith in the creative laws of life,
faith in the goodness of God in the land of the living, faith in the great truth that you know your own
thought is creative. What you feel, you attract, and
what you imagine, you become.

We're not talking about faith in creeds or dogmas
or tradition. Peter, we're told, denied his Lord three
times and said, *"When the cock crows the third time, you
will deny me,"* meaning that you will deny any man as
your master. You will give no allegiance to any church
or any man on the face of the earth, and you will recognize no man as master. You'll recognize God as
master.

Three, the cock crowing, means symbol of dawn, or birth, or light. It is also a symbol of victory, a symbol of triumph, a symbol of conviction. Three is always conviction. If you're absolutely convinced that I Am is the Lord within you, and there is no other Lord, you'll give no allegiance to any man or any institution or any creed or dogma. Your total allegiance will be to the God presence within you, and you'll know no other God.

Where is your faith? Is your faith in the infinite intelligence within you, in the supreme power? If so, you are calling Peter to discipleship.

           •   •   •

James is the righteous judge. "*My judgment,*" he said, "*was his robe and diadem.*" This means when we begin to discipline the faculty called James, we decree wholeness, completeness, and perfection. Our judgment, meaning our conviction, is as a robe based on the truth, and the diadem beauty and perfection.

We ask ourselves, "How is it in God in Heaven?" All is harmony, peace, joy, abundance, security, right action, for that's the infinite spirit within you where all is bliss. Then your verdict is based upon harmony, health, and peace.

The judgment, "*With what judgment ye judge, ye shall be judged.*" The decision or the conclusion you come to about any person, whatever that thought is in your mind, you're creating it in your own mind and your own body and circumstances. That's why you don't judge, for what you judge, you are judged. In other words, you create these in your own mind because you're thinking it and feeling it.

Do you now condemn, criticize, or dwell in the shortcomings of others? If this is true, you're not calling James to discipleship—you're actually building these negative qualities within yourself. We fulfill that which we condemn. We become what we condemn. Look around and you will see ample evidence of this.

Are you incapable of hearing unpleasant things about another? Do you hear and realize only the good for the other? The student of truth disciplining James never gossips, criticizes, condemns, vilifies, or finds fault with people. If he hears gossip and it is true, the student rejects it mentally. He never breathes a word of it.

The Bible says, "To imagine evil against the other is to lie." Begin to call this faculty to discipleship. James is the righteous judge, the right thinking, the right feeling based upon universal laws and principles, based upon the eternal truth.

When there is no opinion, there is no suffering. Where there is no judgment, there's no pain. If the cucumber is bitter, do not eat it. If there are briars or brambles on the road, avoid them. Your judgment is your own conclusion in your mind, and the measure you meet shall be measured unto you again. Whatever you send out comes back to you.

If you send out resentment, antagonism, and hostility, if you're thinking and feeling it and you're building poison pockets in your own subconscious mind, then you're creating havoc in your own life. Therefore you are selfish, really, when you bless the other and see the presence of God in the other and call it forth, because you're blessing yourself.

•   •   •

John is the embodiment of love. Love frees. Love gives. It's the spirit of God. Love has neither height nor depth, neither length nor breadth. It neither comes nor goes, and it fills all space. The ancients said that the world was framed on the shoulders of love.

When you love a woman you don't do anything unloving. Love is kind, it vaunteth not itself. It's not puffed up. Love is not possessiveness. Love is not jealousy. Love is not resentment. Love is trust. When you looked into your mother's eyes, you saw love there. You trusted her. Do you trust your wife and your husband? Are you seeing the God in them?

If you love your wife, you love to see her as she ought to be, happy, joyous, and free. If you love your husband, you love to see him successful, happy, joyous, illumined, inspired. You love to see all the qualities of God resurrected within him, and you pray for him. Likewise, you pray for your wife. You identify with God in the other, and you exalt the God presence in the other. That's loving the other.

We know that *"all things work together for good to them that love God."* "Love God" means give your allegiance, loyalty, devotion to the one presence and the one power, the living spirit within you. The minute you give allegiance to sticks or stones or any created thing, or you put some man on a pedestal, or you worship the stars or the sun or the moon or any created thing, that moment you cease to love God. You're no longer loyal to the one presence and power, for love is loyalty.

"I am God, and there is no God beside me. From the rising of the sun to the setting of the same, there is none else." Therefore, you do not give power to any created thing. The man who loves God does not give power to the phenomenalistic world. He does not give power to a created thing, he gives power to the Creator.

Are you giving all your allegiance, devotion, and loyalty and recognition to the one presence, the living spirit within you? Are you giving power to others to disturb you? Are you giving power to the weather? If someone sneezes, do you give power to the germs? If so, you're not loving John. You're not loving that particular faculty within you.

God and good are identical and synonymous in all sacred scriptures. When we fall in love with qualities and attributes such as honesty, integrity, success, peace, forbearance, and justice, when we love truth for truth's sake, we are loving God and good, for these words are synonymous.

Are you afraid of the future? Are you worried about your family, friends, or business? In short, are you unhappy? If you are, you can rest assured you're not loving God or the good. When you busy your mind with the principles of harmony, right action, beauty, love, peace, and goodwill, then these ideas will sink into your subconscious mind, and the subconscious will bring these qualities forth on the screen of space, for whatever is impressed in your subconscious mind comes forth as form, function, experience, and event.

If you are fearful, worried, and afraid there's not enough to go around, you're emotionally attached to limitation. *"That which I fear most has come upon me."* Are you afraid of failure? If you have this fear, you will bring about failure.

Do we hold a grudge against any living being? If so, we're not calling John to discipleship, for John is love. If this is true, we're not controlling John. We're not calling that faculty to discipleship, because when we discipline these faculties, they will work wonders in our lives. They will become our servants, but if they're undisciplined, they're like an unruly mob.

In order to bring John to discipleship, you must forgive the other. You must forgive yourself for harboring negative, destructive thoughts. Otherwise, there is no love in our hearts. Love the other by rejoicing that the person you say wronged you or cheated you, rejoice that he's living joyously and happily, that the light of God is shining in him.

Claim that the law of God is working for him, through him, and all around him, and that peace fills his mind, body, and affairs. Radiate love, peace, and goodwill to him. Wish for him all the blessings of life. When you do that, you'll realize then that love is the fulfilling of the law, for love is goodwill. It's an out-reaching of the heart. You have to love the other. You don't have to like him.

You don't have to invite him into your home, associate with him, but you do have to love him in the sense that you wish for him health, happiness, and peace and all the blessings of life. That's very simple. You're selfish when you do that, because you're blessing yourself. You're thinking of these things, and you're meditating on them, and you're creating these qualities in your own mind, body, and circumstances.

Can you rejoice in hearing good news about the so-called enemy? If you cannot, you're not in charge of this faculty. If you have failed to embody your ideal, you're not disciplining John, for John is emotional attachment.

You know you can fall in love with music, harmony, electronics. Einstein said he fell in love with the principle of mathematics. Edison fell in love with the principle of electricity and it revealed all its secrets to him, revealed countless inventions to him. He said he picked them up out of the air. Out of the air means from the spirit within him.

Remember love frees, love gives. It's the spirit of God. Love is not emotional blackmail, and if you're clocking your husband or wife when he comes home, there's no love in that home. That's alright in a factory, where you clock in at 9:00 in the morning, but that doesn't belong in any home where love reigns supreme.

There is no love without discipline, no discipline without love. So if you love your children, you'll discipline them. You'll see that they conform to the Golden Rule and the law of love, for there is no love without discipline.

There's no love without wisdom either. Wisdom is an awareness of the presence and power of God where you bring forth these great eternal truths of God in your mind, in your body, and in your circumstances.

•   •   •

Philip means metaphysically a lover of horses. A trainer of horses is firm but kind. He does not beat the horse, yet he lets the horse know that he is master. The trainer is persistent. He has that quality which so many people lack. That is, stick-to-itiveness, determination, persevering to the end.

"He who perseveres to the end shall be saved," meaning the solution shall come to the man who steadfastly gives his attention, devotion, and loyalty to his idea, his dream, his aspiration. He refuses to take no for an answer.

The trainer of a horse is disciplined. He's firm but kind. He throws the horse down, ties his legs with a rope. He talks to the horse, and he lets the horse know that he's the master. He says to the horse, "You'll obey me. I'm going to ride you. You're going to become docile and calm. You're going to become my servant." The horse is subjective, and the subconscious mind is subject to the conscious mind. The conscious mind controls the subconscious.

This is why man has dominion over animals. This is why he can, for example, hypnotize tigers. The tigers are all hypnotized, and then the girls go into the cage, and everybody wonders how. It's because the tigers are all in a subjective state. They're in a trance state because the trainer hypnotized them and said, "You'll obey. You're relaxed. You're at ease," and so on.

After a while, the horse realizes that man is his master because he can thrown him down and tie him up. Eventually, the horse says, "You know, that man is my master." Then the man jumps on his back, and in a docile way, he drives the horse down the road.

The same thing applies to all animals. This is why man has control. This is why he can train a lion or a wolf and so on to do tricks because the subjective is amenable to suggestion. Philip, therefore, is the faculty of mind within us that enables us to use the power we have through love. Thus we conquer any situation.

At a rodeo, you see a horse which is unbridled and untamed. No one can stay on him longer than a few seconds. This is the way with many people. They contemplate a new idea. They become enthused about it. However someone may sway them, or they may hear some unpleasant news which throws them off the horse.

For example, a girl was contemplating a beautiful trip to Italy. She had planned to visit some relatives near Rome. She told some of her girlfriends and others about it, and they said, Oh, don't go to Italy. They hate Americans there. The students are burning the flag, and all this sort of thing. The food is terrible, and the hotels hate you. The money situation is very bad, and all this sort of thing.

She listened to all this talk and canceled the trip. You know, she listened to these girls saying how awful conditions were, that there was no possibility of swimming there, the water was polluted, the prices were outrageous, and all that.

Later, some of her friends went to Italy, and they had the time of their life. Since she had contemplated, you see, a delightful trip, and undoubtedly she would have had a wonderful trip, she lived in the joyous expectancy of it, "As within, so without." A wonderful trip was in store for her, but she permitted the negative suggestions of others to throw her off the lovely horse that she was riding.

"Let us ride the mood to Jerusalem," means let us sustain it, and we will reach the city of peace within ourselves. In other words, it is the sustained mood that creates. You have to be faithful every step of the way to the end.

A trainer of horses is an expert. He's teaching others how to drive the horse, and how to ride the horse, too. One day suddenly he's thrown by a particular horse. What does he do? He doesn't say, "Why did this happen to me? What's wrong with me? I must be losing my grip." Not at all. He jumps on the back of the horse as fast as he can, taps it gently, and off he goes.

He knows very well that if he began to analyze himself and say, "What's wrong with me?" he'd become nervous, irritable, and upset, and the horse would pick it up. He'd lose his cool, so to speak. He'd lose his balance, equilibrium, and serenity. But he's too smart for that. He doesn't spend one moment in regret, and climbs right back up on the horse.

Is that what you do? If so, you are disciplining Philip. Can you be swayed or made to change your mind? Can negative suggestions, ridicule, and criticisms of others throw you off the horse? If this is true, you're not disciplining Philip.

Does the death of one of your dear ones cause you to feel despondent and gloomy, or do you rejoice in their new birthday? If you feel dejected and gloomy, you're not calling Philip to discipleship, but if you rejoice in their birthday, you are.

· · ·

Bartholomew means according to the Concordance, son of the furrowed, or son of the plowed that is prepared for seed. Metaphysically, it represents imagination. Imagination separates man from man. It's the beacon of light in the world of darkness. Government, business, art, and science, they're all looking for men with imagination. The whole world says it can't be done. The man with imagination says it is done.

This faculty of imagination has the power to cast every idea that man can conceive onto the screen of space in substance and form. The disciplined imagination, the furrowed land is capable of picturing only lovely states and delightful moods. Imagination and faith are the two pillars, Jachin and Boaz, that lead to the holy of holies within yourself.

We call Bartholomew to discipleship when we imagine the reality of the fulfilled desire. Whatever you imagine and feel to be true, your subconscious will accept and bring it to pass as form, function, experience, and events.

If you were told of some evil prediction that frightened you, and you begin to imagine and conjure evil, you have not called forth this power. Do not imagine evil for another or for yourself. Do you imagine that your son will fail in his examination or that something bad will happen to members of your family? If you have these negative patterns, you're failing to call this great faculty to discipleship, for imagination is the workshop of God.

Imagine what is lovely, beautiful, and of good report. Imagine you're a tremendous success. Imagine you now are doing what you love to do, divinely happy, divinely prospered.

The great singer imagines she's before a wonderful audience and that the majestic cadences of God are coming forth through her. She imagines loved ones congratulating her. She sees the audience, and she gets the thrill and the joy of seeing a light in their eye and of listening to the applause. She does all that in her mind, and it sinks into the subconscious mind.

The nature of the subconscious is compulsion, and so she's compelled to become the great singer or the great dancer, as the case may be. Imagine what is lovely and of good report.

Perhaps your little boy is at school. What do you imagine about him? Do you think the truck has run over him or that he's fallen into the pond, or that he's gone to get sick or the flu or something? No, you realize where he is, God is, and the love of God surrounds him, enfolds him, and enwraps him.

You're the mother, let us say, and you close your eyes during the day, and the little boy comes home and tells you, "Mother, the teacher praised me today. Look at the wonderful marks I received."

You're imagining what is lovely and of good report, and that's exactly what the boy will do because you're calling things that be not as though they were. The unseen becomes seen because of what you imagine the other telling you, and as you feel the wonders of it all. As you rejoice in that, you are actually calling forth the God in him because the boy is born to win, to succeed.

Therefore imagine whatsoever things are true, lovely, noble, and Godlike. Dwell on these things. If you're married, imagine your husband is coming home telling you what you long to hear, that he's found a wonderful promotion, he's been promoted, that he's found a wonderful job, as the case may be. He's telling you the things you want to hear, how wonderful the day was, how wonderful you are, how much he loves you.

Then see the light in his eyes. See the smile. Hear the tonal qualities of his voice, and feel the divine embrace. Feel the naturalist, the tangibility, the wonders of it all. Make it real, for imagination is called the workshop of God, and I'd like to reiterate that imagination separates man from man. It is a beacon light in a world of darkness.

● ● ●

Thomas means jointed or conjoined. In the undisciplined state, it represents the double-minded man, unstable in all his ways. *"Let not such a man ask anything of the Lord, for he's the double-minded man. He's like the surge of the sea tossed to and fro, a double-minded man, unstable in all his ways."*

Thomas represents the understanding faculty of man. *"Get wisdom. With all thy getting, get understanding."* Wisdom is the awareness of the presence and power of God within you. Understanding is the application of this knowledge to solve your daily problems and grow spiritually.

Our reason and intellectual perception of the truth becomes anointed by the spirit of God. We go from glory to glory. The man who disciplines this faculty is called Thomas, and he's within you, and knows the self-originating spirit is the God of his world and the seat of causation.

In the Bible, Thomas touches the body. *"Put your hands into my side. Who touched me? I feel virtue has gone out of me."* That means you touch this God presence within you,, mentally and spiritually, and immediately the answer comes. When disciplined, Thomas, that faculty within you, rejects all rumors, lies, and suggestions that are unlike order or the truth.

He will contradict, reject, and refuse to accept any rumors or suggestions that oppose that which he knows to be true. For example, if there's an epidemic of the flu or whatever it might be, he's unmoved, undisturbed. He realizes that there's only one presence, one power, one cause, and one substance. So his prayer is, "I am all health. God is my health." He builds up an immunity or spiritual antibodies and contravenes against everything that man believes, against all the opinions of the world, and he has just the one Lord, the one power, the one cause, the one substance.

Do you send your children to some remote spot to escape the so-called flu or Asian flu or something else? If this is true about you, you're full of fear. Your faith is not in God or good, and you do not believe in the omnipresence of God. If you're calling Thomas to discipleship, you'll realize that you're always in your true place, that you're in the secret place of the most high, that you abide in the shadow of the Almighty. You'll say of the Lord he's your refuge, your fortress. *"My God, in Him will you trust."*

You know that God is where you stand, that he walks and talks in you. You are the very garment which God wears as he moves through the illusion of time and space. You discipline Thomas when you touch reality, and you know that God is the only presence, power, cause, and substance.

Therefore a plague could be sweeping the city, and you would be completely unmoved and undisturbed because you realize you're sealed in God, and nothing could touch you. That would be a wonderful attitude of mind to develop.

* * *

Matthew means the gift of Jehovah. It means your desire, and God speaks to man through the medium of desire. For example, if you're sick, you desire health. If you're hungry, you want food, and if you're in prison, you want freedom. If you're thirsty, you want water. Realization of your desire would be your savior. It would be the solution to your problem.

Therefore God speaks to you through desire, and there's a desire in you as you listen to this, the spirit within you, the life principle saying, "Come on up higher. I have need of you." Therefore, if you're beginning to discipline Matthew, you will say, "Well, God gave me this desire. This desire is good and very good, and the same living spirit Almighty which gave me this desire will reveal the perfect plan for its unfoldment and divine order through divine love."

You will take this desire of yours and you'll animate it, sustain it, exalt it, lift it up in your mind, marshal all the reasons why you can accomplish it, why you can achieve it. You don't discuss it with others. Go tell no man—show John. You don't discuss your prayer life, your dreams, your aspirations, your plans, your purposes with others.

When you do, many times they'll tell you all the reasons why you can't achieve them. So tell them nothing. Prayer is a silent communion, a dialog with your higher self. It's a secret commitment whereby you dwell on the reality of your desire, and you realize the power of the Almighty is moving on your behalf and that the desire will come to pass in divine order through divine love, just the same as you put a seed in the ground. The seed undergoes dissolution bequeathing its energy to another form of itself.

Likewise, as you envelope your desire with faith and confidence, knowing there's an Almighty power that will bring it to pass, that desire will be deposited in your subconscious mind. It will die as a desire and come forth as the joy of the answered prayer.

Do you say, "I am too old, I lack the intelligence, It's too late now, I have no chance?" Do you accept the verdict of the doctor, or the mass mind belief? Or do you go within and say like Mary of old, "My soul doth magnify the Lord?"

Go within the silence, and magnify the possibility of realizing that desire. You will magnify the possibility of giving birth to your idea, dream, or aspiration. Nourish it, sustain it, exalt it, love it, woo it, and gradually as you walk with it, you're conditioning your mind, realizing that the Almighty power is backing you up. It will sink into your subconscious where it will die. When it dies, then comes, as I said, the joy of the answered prayer.

When you reject your desire, the gift of God which would bless you in the world, you're not calling Matthew to discipleship. For the desire that you now have to be the great artist, the great singer, or the great pianist, as the case may be, you can rest assured that the desire that lingers is the true desire. And if you have an intense desire to paint or sing or play music, that means that the talent is there, and when the talent is there, the way is there.

You can make a seed grow. The oak is already in the acorn, but you have to deposit it in the soil. The archetype or the pattern is already there. It dies in the soil and attracts everything it needs for its unfoldment. Likewise, you know when you've turned your request over to the deeper mind, because when you've turned it over to your subconscious full of wisdom and intelligence, it has the know-how of accomplishment.

You're at peace. You're no longer anxious or worried. You're not saying how, when, and where, or, "How long, oh Lord, how long?" If you do, you're not disciplining Matthew, for Matthew trusts the God presence like you delegate an assignment to an officer in the company.

If you're a good executive, you don't meddle with the pie you ask the other man to make, do you? You trust the other man. You gave him an assignment. He's capable, he's competent. Likewise, whatever you impress on that subconscious mind will move Heaven and Earth to bring to pass, but all the wisdom of the infinite are within you.

* * *

James the Less signifies the faculty of order or a tidy mind. Order is Heaven's first law. When you are at peace in your mind, when you find peace in your home, in your business and in the rest of your affairs, then you're calling that faculty to discipleship. James the Less is also called discernment or discrimination. It also means clairvoyance, clairaudience, or perceiving the truth about anything.

Quimby, the father of metaphysics in America and the greatest healer America has ever known, had a highly developed quality of discernment. He was able to diagnose and interpret all the causes behind the ailments or maladies of his patients. His patients didn't have to tell him anything. He saw the cause of their sickness, whether it was consumption, cancer, tuberculosis, blindness or insanity, whatever it might be.

He told them where their pains and aches were and the mental patterns behind them. Over sixty percent of his patients were sick because of religious beliefs, a punitive God, a belief in a Hell, damnation, that they were sinners, and so on.

Today we go to a doctor and we tell him all of our symptoms, their location, and so forth, but Quimby did the reverse. He told the patient the cause of his malady and where it was, and they marveled at this great capacity. He simply tuned in on their subconscious minds and subjectively saw their mental patterns. His explanation was the cure.

Quimby was clairvoyant. When this clairvoyant faculty is fully developed, one sees the divinity behind the form, the truth behind the mask. He contemplates reality and sees the presence of God everywhere.

How did Quimby become clairvoyant? By discarding all the theological beliefs he was taught when he was young. He rejected all the opinions of man, and he recognized that there was only one presence and power within himself. A good book to read is *Psychic Perception*, one of my recent books dealing with extrasensory perception. It tells you how to develop these faculties.

Do you blame the government, external conditions, family, employers, or conditions for any problems or limitations you may be experiencing? It is easy to blame others. Are you capable of interpreting that which you see? Do you judge according to appearances? Objective appearance is not always true.

Call James the Less to discipleship. "*Let your judgment be as the noonday. Noon casts no shadow. I stand in my shadow, therefore nothing comes in my way to deflect me from judging righteously.*" No shadow must cross your path. The world of confusion shall be rejected. Your judgment shall be righteousness, which is wholeness and perfection, perfect God, perfect man, and perfect being.

Your judgment is based upon what's true of God, just like an engineer. How does he base his judgment? On the laws of stress and strain, pressure, and the principle of mathematics. Therefore he can tell you that a train weighing so many tons can pass over this particular bridge. It's all computed mathematically, all done scientifically. He's judging righteously according to universal principles and laws.

Nothing will give you peace but the triumph of principles, and your mind is a principle. If you think good, then good follows. If you think evil, then evil follows.

If you want to develop the faculties of sight and hearing within you, clairvoyance and clairaudience, say to yourself:

"I see the truth. I love the truth. I know the truth. I rejoice in the truth. By day and by night, I am seeing more and more of God's truths spiritually, mentally, materially, and every single way. That spirit of truth leads me to all truth."

Realize that you're illumined from on high. The spirit of Almighty God moves in the waters of your mind. All your faculties are illuminated from on high. The light of God shines in all the dark places of your mind, *"For they that dwelt in darkness have seen a great* light. *They that dwelt in the valley of the shadow, upon them hath the light shineth.*"

The wisdom of God anoints your intellect. "*It's a lamp unto your feet. It's a light upon your path.*" You're seeing more and more of God's truth every moment of the day. You see the divinity behind the form and the truth behind the mask. Then, you are disciplining James the Less. Intuitively, you will perceive the great truths of God without any conscious process or reasoning.

* * *

Thaddeus means of the heart, warmhearted, and praise. Thaddeus represents the exalted mood and the happy, joyous state. "*I, if I be lifted up from the earth, will draw all men unto me.*" If you take that idea you have and lift it up to the point of acceptance or conviction in your own mind, the manifestation will come to you. It will appear on the screen of space, for anything that you completely accept in your mind will come to pass.

This is the attitude of the mind of the man who's disciplining Thaddeus. It means praise, exaltation. The Bible says, "*Come into His presence singing. Come into His courts with praise. Be thankful unto Him, and bless His name.*"

It's a quality sadly lacking in the minds of millions of people. Do you praise your boy for a job well done?

Do you praise your assistant or associate for marvelous, constructive work? It would be a wonderful thing to do. Do you praise the waitress for the excellent service she gave you?

Exalt God in the midst of the other person. If you have a little boy or a little girl, you can exalt God in the midst of the child. For example, the little girl may be at school, but you can say, "The wisdom of God anoints my girl's mind. She's growing in grace and wisdom, truth and beauty. The love of God wells up within her. The peace of God floods her mind. She's illumined from on high."

If you have a little boy, you can realize infinite intelligence is within him, guiding and directing him, revealing to him his hidden talents, showing him the way he should go, realizing the love, the light, and the glory of the infinite animate and sustain him and strengthen him, and that he is God's son expressing more and more of God every day.

You're praising, exalting, and lifting up the God in the boy, and he will become to you what you conceive him to be. He will fulfill your conviction of him. *Never have I seen the righteous forsaken.* The righteous are those think right, feel right, act right, and who use the law in the right way.

We lift others up by rejoicing that they're now possessing and expressing all that we long to see them express. You can praise the flowers in the flowerpot that's grown for hundreds and thousands of years, and they will grow luxuriously and beautifully. Ask the little geranium plant to bend over and kiss you. It will. It will grow toward you so that you may kiss it, just as a dog will jump on your lap just as you indicate you will pet him.

Do we lift others up in consciousness and see them as they ought to be seen? Do you see men as beggars? If that is true, we have clothed them in rags, but the so-called beggar is a king walking the king's highway. Clothe him with the garment of salvation. Clothe him with the garment of righteousness. Realize the riches of God are flowing through him, that he's illumined from on high.

If you have a good conviction, the beggar will be transformed. He will not be at the street corner tomorrow. This is an example of calling Thaddeus to discipleship. The ancients said, *"Thaddeus went forth on the earth; his neck and head bathed with oil."* Oil means illumination and inspiration. It means the light of God. They said, *"All those who touched him remained whole, that he went forth with the praise of God forever on his lips."*

Praise radiates and gives glory and beauty to the inner powers of man, that assimilate Thaddeus and walk the earth with the praise of God forever on your lips. Then you're really calling Thaddeus to discipleship.

Likewise, if you give thanks for the blessings you have now, count your blessings. The wonderful home, the blessings of your husband, your wife, your children, your health, your eyesight. Some people can't see, some can't hear. You give thanks for all the wonderful blessings you have now and *"exalt God in the midst of you, might He to heal."*

Then you'll see your subconscious will magnify your good exceedingly, and wonders will happen in your life. *"Father, he said, I thank thee that thou hast heard me, and I know that thou healest me always."* The ancient poets said, *"Oh, God give me one more thing, a grateful heart."* Praise and gratitude are wonderful qualities.

* * *

Another disciple is Simon of Canaan. Simon means hearing, heartening. It means one who listens and obeys the voice of the one who forever is. Simon is "to hear," Canaan is the Promised Land. The Promised Land is the realization of your heart's desires, the fruition of your ideas.

When a scientist has an invention, when it comes forth and is objectified and made manifest, he has reached the Promised Land, hasn't he? When we discipline this faculty, we look for and expect spiritual guidance and illumination direct from the fountainhead of God. We become still and listen for the small voice, the vibration or tone within us that wells up and says, "This is the way. Walk ye in."

Simon is also the man with the pitcher of water, and you're told to follow that man, and he will lead you to an upper room where everything is prepared. What is this upper room? It's the presence of God in you, the living spirit Almighty. It was never born, it will never die. "*Water wets it not, fire burns it not, wind blows it not away.*"

Love was never born, and it will never die. It never grows old. Grace never grows old. Joy never grows old, and beauty never grows old. Laughter never grows old. These are eternal qualities. Harmony always was, now is, and ever shall be. These are qualities, attributes, and potencies of God.

The Kingdom of Heaven is at hand, and the works are finished from the foundation of time. "*All things be ready if the mind be so,*" for the works are finished. You're dealing with the finished kingdom. No matter what you seek already is, because, "*Before you call, I will answer.*"

Therefore, no matter what the question is, the solution is already there. The answer is there, whether it's to the scientist or the man lost in the woods or the doctor seeking a solution. The answer is already there. That's why it is an insult to the divinity within you to beg, beseech, or supplicate. That's why you go boldly to the throne of grace. You claim your good, which was given to you from the foundation of time.

So you go into that upper room, and you realize harmony is. You don't say, "It takes a long time to get a healing." You're saying God takes a long time to heal. You don't say, "Some day I'll be happy and some day I'll have peace." The God of peace is within you. Tune in on the God of peace and let the river of peace flow through you now. You don't say, "Some day I'll have love." The God of love is within you. Open your mind and heart and let God's love flow through you. The answer is now, for God, your good, is the eternal now.

Simon of Canaan may be summed up as receptivity. To the inner voice of wisdom, truth, and beauty, this leads us to the land of Canaan, the Promised Land, the realization of harmony, health, and peace.

We hear only the good news about ourselves and others. We expect the best, and invariably, the best will come to you because you expect it. The man who disciplines his faculty of mind lives in a state of joyous expectancy. The best invariably comes to him.

The word of God goes before such a man as a pillar of a cloud to lead him on the way, and by night in a pillar of fire to give him light. By day and by night.

Do you gossip, dissect others, criticize them, and indulge in backbiting? These negative qualities prevent you from controlling and disciplining this important faculty of mind. Do you hear and feel only the best for others? If you can, "*Turn not aside and faint not, and this presence and power will lead you to a land of plenty, flowing with the milk of life eternal and the honey of unblemished wisdom.*"

"*The pillar of cloud will lead you on the way, and by night in the pillar of fire.*" The ancients took a razor, a metallic instrument where you put coal in, when they wandered in the desert. Some of them got lost but they would see the smoke during the day, and they would follow where the smoke was. At night the sparks would fly upwards, and even though they were lost, they would see the sparks, and they would go towards the sparks.

That has an inner meaning. The cloud by day, as clouds become saturated and fall as rain. "*I'll rain blessings from Heaven for you.*" It means walk in the consciousness of God's presence. The love of God surrounds you, enfolds you, and enwraps you. In divine love going before you, that's the pillar of cloud.

Pillar is a fixed conviction of God's presence. That leads you on the way, "*For divine love goes before you, making straight, joyous, and glorious your way.*" At night you may be sound asleep upon the bed, but God makes Himself known in a vision and will speak to you in a dream.

• • •

Judas means limitation, the sense of need, desire, or the unredeemed life forces. It has nothing to do with a man, it's not a man at all. We're all born with Judas, because that's the only way you can develop and discover yourself. You must have problems, challenges, and difficulties, otherwise you'd never discover your divinity. You're not born fully armed. God becomes man by His belief in being man. God limits Himself by His belief in being man. Therefore, you are God walking the earth.

You have a body; you're limited. You're born into all that this mass mind represents. We're born into the world where we're conscious of boundaries, time, distance, and other limitations. You're aware of opposites, you're a sensing being. You have sensation, and there's night and day, ebb and flow, in and out, sweet and sour. There's comparisons, and so on.

"Thou hast been in Eden, the garden of God; every precious stone was thy covering." We were all in a desireless state at one time. We were in the living spirit Almighty. Then we're born into the three-dimensional world, and we have desires. Our failure to realize our desires, cherished hopes, and ideals is the cause of our frustration.

Lack of understanding has caused men to lust, hate, and be greedy for other people's property, territory, possessions, and land. So it is said Judas carried the bag of money, the sense of need, or limitation. When we discipline this faculty it is one of the greatest of all the disciples, for it reveals the God self, the truth that sets us free.

We are told Judas betrayed Jesus. This is a parable, an allegory. *Betray* in the Bible means to reveal, so I must know your secret. The secret is the presence of God in you. Every problem reveals its own solution in the form of a desire. An eight year old boy can see this.

Judas is necessary for the drama. *"I have chosen 12, and one of you is the devil,"* meaning limitation. You can't get rid of it because it's necessary for your unfoldment, but it's through our problems we discover the God presence within, which is our savior. The joy is in overcoming the problems. When we accept our desire, then the realization of our desire is our Jesus, or the solution to our problem. All of that is symbolic.

Judas dies or commits suicide, and the savior or answered prayer is revealed or made manifest. We discipline Judas when we surrender ourselves to the influx of divine love and consecrate ourselves to the purity of purpose. When we realize our oneness with all mankind, we die to all the false beliefs of the world.

When we give up all this brainwashing and the false beliefs which were inculcated into our cranium, divine love overcomes all problems and transforms man into the pure, original state.

Have we any religious political prejudices now, personal saviors, or things of that nature? Do you look down on others and say, "It's unfortunate that they're not Christians?" If so you're not disciplining this faculty, for God is no respecter of persons, knows nothing about Jews or Christians. *"In Him there's no Jew, no Greek,"* and no Hindu, nor anything else. Only the ever-flowing reality, flowing on forever.

Do you like to retain your prejudices? If this is true, you're not disciplining Judas, because Judas means attachment, which is the divine indifference. Indifference is the tie that severs. You detach yourself from all these beliefs, and you'll realize there's only one God, the Father of all, and we're all God's children.

Love is that which binds us to our good, which means that we take our attention away from that which we do not want, and focus it on the good that we do. When we die to all false beliefs, we're back again in the Garden of God. *"Thou hast been in Eden, the Garden of God."*

When a man who's poverty stricken dies to that false belief, and he becomes a multimillionaire employing thousands. His Judas committed suicide. He died to his false beliefs about God, and he resurrected a God of opulence.

"In Him there is neither Jew nor Greek, neither bond nor free, neither male nor female." So as the sun moves through the zodiac in its cycle, in like manner must the spirit of God move through our 12 faculties, symbolically speaking, inspiring and breathing into them the life of the one presence and the one power.

As we discipline these faculties, we consciously become God's radiation, dissolving barriers between men. Realize that you're here to glorify God and enjoy Him forever. "I glorify thee on earth that I finish the work which thou gavest me to do. Glorify thou me with thine own self, with the glory which I had with thee right now."

The Supreme
Mastery of Fear

Keep on telling your subconscious mind that I and my Father are one, that one with God is a majority, and if God be for me, who can be against me? The life principle is always for you. It heals a cut on your finger. If you took some bad food, it causes you to regurgitate it. You burned yourself, it reduces the edema. It gives you new skin and tissue. It always seeks to preserve you and to heal and restore you. Keep telling your subconscious you are divine.

Your subconscious wants you to say it over and over again, for ideas are conveyed to the subconscious by repetition, faith, and expectancy. Do it again and again and again, and realize that the God presence is within you and that you're one with it, that you're divine. You're a son of the living God. You're heir to all of God's riches and all the power of the gotten flows to your focal point of attention.

Tell yourself that over and over again and gradually your subconscious will accept it. Your subconscious will believe it because you're believing it in your conscious, reasoning mind, and whatever your conscious mind really believes, your subconscious will dramatize and bring to manifestation.

Do not vacillate or equivocate. Your subconscious mind knows when you are sincere. It knows when you really believe, and then it will respond. Tell yourself frequently that God indwells you, that you are divine, that omnipotence is moving on your behalf. Say it to yourself when you're challenged. When you have any kind of a trouble or difficulty, say, "This is divinely outmatched. The problem is here, but the God presence is here, too."

Say it to yourself when you're driving the car, when you're going to sleep, when you're talking to someone. Realize God is thinking, speaking, acting through you, and realize it is always functioning. When fear comes, say, "Faith in God opens the door of your mind, and there's no one there."

Realize that you are one with this God power. You're aligned with it now, and mighty forces will come to your aid. You are one with the infinite, with life, and with all things. The Bible says, *"Thou shall compass me about with songs of deliverance. I will fear no evil, for thou art with me. Thy rod and thy staff may comfort me. Goodness and mercy follow me all the days of my life, for I dwell in the house of God forever."* Your mind is the house of God. It's where you walk and talk with the supreme intelligence, with this infinite presence and power.

When you are fearful or indulge in negative thoughts, you're vibrating at a very low level. When you meditate on a psalm, say to yourself, "The Lord is my shepherd, I shall not want," or, "The presence of God is right where I am," or, "I will fear no evil, for God is with me," or, "I dwell in the secret place of the most high, and I abide in the shadow of the Almighty. I will say of the Lord, He's my refuge, my fortress. My God, in Him will I trust. Surely, He will cover me with His feathers, and under His wings shall I rest. The truth shall be my shield and buckler."

Affirm frequently, "God is guiding me now. The presence of God is with me." Then you're thinking spiritually. Your thoughts are now God's thoughts, and all the power of God flows through that thought. That's the meaning of one with God as a majority, for the only immaterial power is your thought, and your thought is creative. Think of harmony, think of infinite love flowing through you, vitalizing, healing, restoring you. These spiritual thoughts are of a very high frequency and are of a very high vibration.

What happens to the evil, negative thoughts of fear, foreboding, destruction, disaster, earthquakes, things of this nature? As when you say, "Oh, maybe another earthquake will come, maybe my house will be knocked down." Instead say, "God's love surrounds me, enfolds me. The presence of God is in my home which is the presence of harmony, beauty, love, and peace. Divine love saturates the walls, the atmosphere."

Wherever you are, whether asleep or awake, walking the streets or behind the counter, God's love surrounds you, enfolds you, and enwraps you. You're immunized, you're God-intoxicated, you have no fear. You're not afraid of anything in the past, the present, or the future. You're not afraid of people, conditions, or events. For the eternal God is your dwelling place, and underneath of the everlasting arms of wisdom is truth and beauty.

You're immersed in the holy omnipresence. In Him we live and move and have our being, and this God presence lives, moves, and has its being in us. Now you're vibrating at a spiritual frequency, and just like you put your finger on a tuning fork, that is the end of the negative or fearful vibration. That is the end of the evil, because evil is a false belief about the infinite one, and the infinite goodness of the infinite one.

When we are full of fear, we have greater faith in evil than in the God presence. Shocking, but it's true. Fear is God upside down. You have faith that the sun will rise in the morning. You have faith that you can drive your car. You have faith that you will get an answer to your prayer when you pray for guidance, but many people have faith in the wrong thing.

There are people who are looking forward to misfortune. There are people working in offices who are afraid of their jobs. They're afraid they're going to lose their money and what's going to happen to them when they grow old instead of realizing, "I'm always in my true place. God is the source of my supply, and all my needs are met at every moment of time and point of space. God is my instant, everlasting supply, meeting all my needs. At every moment of time, no matter where I am, I am always gainfully employed. I'm always working for him, and I live forever."

·   ·   ·

Why be upset, angry, or fearful at another's remark? Does what the other man says contribute to your success, to your happiness, your peace, or your failure in any way? No. His thought has no power. Your power is with your thoughts of good.

Someone may spread lies about you, and you say, "They're undermining me, they're telling lies about me." You're full of fear and anger, but does their opinion make it so? No.

What governs you? Your belief or another's belief? Your thought or someone else's? Do you own your own mind, or are you permitting others to manipulate you? Who's thinking for you?

Are you coming to your own decisions? Are you doing your own thinking? You are in the Kingdom of Heaven. The Kingdom of Heaven means you're king over your conceptive realm which is your own mind. You have authority. You have dominion over your thoughts and feelings, emotions, and action.

That's why the Kingdom of Heaven is within you. It's not a place up in the skies where you go—you're already there. Why make yourself subservient to another person's thought? Why not have reverence for your own thought? Your thought is divine. It is creative. It is of God.

This capacity of spirit is to think, and you're a spirit now. You'll always be a spirit. When were you not a spirit? Quimby said that in 1845. Have a healthy, reverent respect for your thought because your thought is your prayer. What you feel, you attract. What you imagine, you become. Your thought governs you, not another.

Stand tall and straight and say, "I'm one with the infinite, which lies stretched in smiling repose. The finite alone hath rot and suffered, but the infinite lies stretched in smiling repose."

Each time a fear thought comes to you, supplant it and say, "God loves me and cares for me. I'm surrounded by the sacred circle of God's eternal love." Paul says, *"The whole armor of God surrounds me and enfolds me and enwraps me, and divine love goes before me making straight and perfect my way."*

A pilot said to me, "I'm never afraid when I navigate a plane, whether I go north, south, east, or west, for I'm a pilot for God. I am flying for Him. I am as safe in the sky as on the earth. Nothing can happen to me. It is impossible. I'm always surrounded by the sacred circle of God's eternal love."

Have faith in the goodness of God, the right action of God, and the guidance of that infinite one within you. Have faith in the eternal principle and in the immutable, changeless laws of God. Have faith in your own mind because any idea that you emotionalize, nourish, sustain, or exalt in your mind, it sinks down into your subconscious by the process of osmosis, where it dies like a seed and bequeaths its energy to another form of itself.

What is the energy that it bequeaths? The joy of the answered prayer. Because after all, the corn or wheat must die before we have a harvest. The apple seed must die before we have an apple. Likewise, your desire is a gift of God, and therefore God does not mock you. You say, God who gave me this desire reveals the perfect plan for its enfoldment. You contemplate the end.

Faith is your attitude of mind. Faith is your thought. Whatever you impress in your subconscious is expressed on the screen of space. Nowhere in any Bible of the world does it say you have to have faith in Catholicism, Buddhism, Judaism, Hinduism, Shintoism, or any -ism. You have faith in the creative laws of your own mind. You have faith in the goodness of God in the land of the living. You have faith that there's an infinite intelligence that responds to your thought. It'll respond to an atheist, agnostic—anybody—and before you call, the answer is there. It was always there.

Faith is what you expect, what you're focused on. The things that you're vividly imagining, they will come to pass. Some people are afraid of old age. Age is not the flight of years, it's the dawn of wisdom.

Some are afraid of death. Death is simply a new birth. That's all that is. You go to sleep every night. That's where you go when men call you dead, in their ignorance.

People are afraid of things that do not exist. You're alive, and your life is God's life. You're alive now. God is life eternal. Because God lives, you live. God cannot die. Therefore, you cannot die. Realize God is your employer, and this God presence is always taking care of you.

The great dancer says, "I dance for Him." The great singer says, "God sings in majestic cadences through me." He commands that internal power and wisdom. He calls upon it, and it answers him. Naturally, he gets honors, he gets emoluments, he gets the praise of his fellow men, but he doesn't seek it. He turns to the source, and all these things are added to him.

"Seek ye first the Kingdom of God," and all these things like honors, wealth, and everything else will be added to you automatically. You'll never want for anything.

*   *   *

When someone makes a negative statement about you, remember, *"I will fear no evil, for thou art with me. Thy rod and thy staff, they comfort me. Perfect love casted out fear, for fear hath torment. He that feareth is not made perfect in love."*

A fearful person is always very selfish. They're wrapped up in themselves, hugging the shore. Love is always outgoing, it is an emanation. Fear is turning within, in morbid introspection, believing someone is going to hurt you or that evil spirits can possess you. All this is ignorance, and ignorance is the only sin. All of this punishment is the consequence of that ignorance. Ignorance is the only devil in the world.

When any person believes in external powers, he denies the one, true cause which moves as a unity. It is the life principle within you, forever seeking to express itself as love, bliss, joy, and right action.

When we are fearful, we are selfish in the wrong way. Fear is a morbid introspection. Cease building a wall around yourself, saying, "I'm going to get hurt." Realize God *is*, and all there is, is God. Realize the love of God surrounds you, enfolds you, and enwraps you.

Say to yourself, "God walks and talks in me. I know I am one with my Father, and my Father is God. I have faith in God. Therefore, I fear not. 'Fear not little flock, for it is your Father's good pleasure to give you the kingdom.'"

Realize you're surrounded by divine love, that God's power is with your thoughts of good, that you're immersed in the only omnipresence. God be with you.

•   •   •

The fear of the Lord is the beginning of wisdom. When you learn the laws of electricity, you're very careful how you apply them because you know the consequences. You know when you put your hand on a naked wire or cause a short circuit what will happen. You learn the theories about insulation, conductivity, resulting in a healthy respect and reverence for these laws. You follow the nature of the principles.

Likewise, when you learn the principle of chemistry, you have a very healthy respect for the combination of chemicals, their atomic weight, because you know the disastrous consequences of mixing things together when you don't know the results. For instance, if you mix nitric acid and glycerin, you will create a powerful explosive.

Fear is reverence, a healthy respect. You have a healthy respect for the law of your mind when you learn the consequences of misusing it, because your mind is a principle. "Nothing can give you peace but the triumph of principles," Emerson said.

You have a healthy respect for fire, so you don't put your finger in it. Similarly, when men know that their mind is a principle, like the principles of chemistry and physics, they have a very healthy respect for the subconscious mind. A principle doesn't change. God is the living spirit within you, it's infinite intelligence and boundless wisdom. It's the only cause, power, or substance in the world. It's supreme and omnipotent. There's nothing to oppose it, nothing to challenge it. Nothing to vitiate it.

If there were two powers, there'd be two wills. There'd be chaos everywhere. There'd be no order, symmetry, or proportion anywhere. When you think

God's thoughts, God's power is with your thoughts of good. You can tune in on the infinite. The only immaterial power you know is your thought.

* * *

"In the beginning was the Word. The Word was with God, and the Word was God."

The Word is a thought expressed. When you have discovered the power of your thought, you've discovered God in that sense, because your thought is creative. Not because it's your thought, but because it *is* thought.

You can demonstrate that under hypnosis, where you can put a finger on a man's neck and say, "This is a red-hot poker." He gets a blister, so you know very well that your thoughts become flesh, become manifest in your life. So you'd better have a healthy respect for your thoughts.

Water runs downhill. It expands when frozen. It takes the shape of any vessel in which it is poured. These and many other characteristics determine the principle by which water operates. Your mind operates in the same way. If you think good, then good follows. If you think evil, evil follows. Evil is the misuse of the law, a misinterpretation of life.

There's only one power, and that's the living spirit Almighty, which is undifferentiated, undefined, the self-originating spirit. Your mind is creative. That is, the thought in your mind is creative. Therefore if you think good, good follows. If you think evil, evil follows. If you say, "The infinite presence can heal me now," it will respond to you.

You can say, "Infinite intelligence guides and directs me and watches over me in all my ways." Faith is an attitude of mind. Faith is the use you make of your mind. Realize that fear is a thought in your own mind, created by yourself. It has no reality, it's a shadow in your mind. The thing you're afraid of does not exist.

Fear is faith in the wrong thing. Fear is faith upside down. Fear is God upside down. It's a twisted, morbid concept of life. The fear of something has the same physiological effect as if it were real.

Say a boy were in a chair and you told him a boogeyman was downstairs with a black bag and was going to take him away because he was a bad boy. Now he's frozen to the chair. He gets white and rigid, and yet there's no reality to the thought. Then take him downstairs, point out to him there's no boogeyman and he's free of the fear. But it had the same physiological and physical effect as if it were real.

* * *

Basil King, who wrote *Conquest of Fear*, tells that he was going blind. He was a young man, depressed and dejected. He feared the future, blindness, and old age. He said he recalls something that a teacher said years ago. "The life principle, which is God in you, is indestructible, invulnerable, and eternal. It always brings about the expedient, which is an answer to the particular need of any man."

He used to think that nature was cruel and raw and that evil abounded in the world. He had strange concepts of God. I might say that good and evil are the movements of your own mind relative to the one being, that it's forever whole, pure, and immaculate in itself. It's the use that you make of the power.

How do you use electricity? You can use it to kill a man or to fry an egg. How do you use nitric acid? You can use it to blind a man, or you can paint a Madonna on a windowpane. How do you use water? To drown a child or quench his thirst? Surely these things are not inherently evil. The forces of nature are not evil. The living spirit is the God presence in you. How are you using it?

This man Basil King who was going blind, he said he used to think that nature was cruel and raw, that God was punishing him. This man said a woman asked him, "What do you think God is?"

He replied, in his simplicity and immaturity and naiveté, "There are three supernal beings in the sky and three thrones." She laughed out loud at him.

"I knew at that moment, I had the wrong concept," he said. Then he began to think of the life principle within him, how it had overcome every obstacle in the world, whether a flood, volcanic eruption, war, destruction of all kinds.

The life principle goes on, invulnerable and eternal. You can't destroy life. Life just is. You're alive. Your life is God. The life principle gives fur to the animals in the North. In the South, in the temperate zone, it gives them hair. It covers others with shells to preserve them. Others are given the poisonous fluid which they emit when attacked. It takes care of all forms of life such as those that came out of the sea. It gave them legs, made them stand upright, gave them wings to fly in the air.

The life principle always meets the particular need. When primitive man met the tiger, he was frozen with fear. Gradually, there came to his aid the dawn of reason, imagination, and memory. There was a time when man had no memory. Later, man began to think, and this power within him responded to his thought.

Basil King, meditating and musing on the power within him, discovered that the natural principle of life and nature is not cruel, and when he combined or united with this principle in thought, mighty forces came to his aid. He no longer believed in three old men sitting on a throne, Father, Son, and Holy Ghost, but he perceived that God was the life principle.

The Trinity is your spirit, your mind, and your body, or spirit, mind, and function, because you need a body to express things. The mind is the priest, or the mediator between the invisible and the visible, namely your own thought. The spirit then responds to the nature of your thought.

The average man has pigeonholed this God presence and brings it out on Sundays, holidays, and in cases of death, birth, and marriage, but for the rest of the time, the God presence is put away in the corner.

Some men are afraid to use the term God. Others look askance when God is mentioned, as they begin to think of God in terms of religious connotations because each has a different concept of God.

God is your mind, your spirit. God is your thought too, because your thought is creative. I say have a healthy respect for it. Think of harmony, of peace, of love, of right action, of beauty. Think of an infinite healing presence. Think that you're surrounded by the sacred circle of God's eternal love. Imagine you're in the midst of the circle, a circle of love, of peace, of harmony, and of power. Nothing will touch you.

You're immunized. You're God-intoxicated. You're always in the sacred center of God's eternal love.

So Basil King discarded all the sentimental, preternatural connotations associated with the name of the deity. He began to realize that God was the life principle within him, the spirit, the mind operating through him. When he united with this infinite intelligence, mighty forces came to his aid. He found this creative intelligence was the answer to every problem.

"This realization was the beginning of the process of casting out fear," he said, "which was blinding me and paralyzing me." No man can conquer fear until he comes back to the fact that there's only one power, one presence, one cause, one substance.

Therefore, you better get it straight in your cranium that the minute you give attention to externals, you're denying the one presence, the one power, because a scientific thinker does not make a created thing greater than the creator. Get it clear and straight in your mind that never again will you give power to any person, place, or thing, condition or circumstance, star or sun or moon or weather or water or anything in this universe to harm, hurt, or bless you.

You simply recognize there's only one creative power. That is the spirit and the mind in you. It's Almighty, over all, through all, and in all. It's the only cause. It's supreme and omnipotent. There's nothing to oppose it. Will you tell me what can oppose omnipotence? Is there something? Show it to me. Let me look at it. It has no reality, it's a shadow in your mind.

Fear is a conglomeration of sinister shadows. You're fighting a shadow in your mind. You're the creator of your own fears, these fears have no reality. Come back to the one presence and the one power, and when you reject and refuse to believe that any person, place, or thing, condition or circumstance can hurt or harm you, then you're on the way. That's your great rejection.

Then comes the great affirmative:

"I am God, and there is no God beside me from the rising of the sun to the setting of the same, there is none else. I am the Lord, thy God. My glory you shall not give to another. Neither shall you give my praise. I am the Lord, thy God, that brought thee out of the land of Egypt, out of the house of bondage."

"There is no other God before me. I Am, and there is none else. The Lord is my light and my salvation."

"Whom shall I fear? The Lord is the strength of my life. Of whom shall I be afraid? For in times of trouble, He will hide me in His pavilion; in the secret of His tabernacle shall he hide me."

"He shall set me up upon a rock, the rock of truth. The same yesterday, today, and forever."

Are you standing on that rock? It's all powerful, all wise, the ever-living one, the all-wise one, the all-knowing one.

No wonder this woman laughed at King when he said there were three supernal beings up in the sky. You are the Trinity yourself. You are the triangle, and you are the circle. The triangle is the spirit, mind, and body, or spirit, mind, and function. You are this being. There's only one power, one presence, and its source is love. It has no opposition.

It is the life principle that has overcome every opposition in this world and goes on conquering. There is nothing to oppose it. It is omnipotent. "I was made to rule," Thoreau said. "Men are born to succeed, not to fail." You're born to win. How could the infinite within you fail? Meditate on this, and accept it.

The Bible says, "Eat the body, and drink the blood," a figurative, idiomatic expression. To eat the body is to eat of the idea, to absorb it, digest it, exalt it, reflect upon it, appropriate it mentally like you'd eat a piece of bread. It becomes tissue, muscle, and bone. It becomes blood.

Delight in this idea that you're born to succeed, that you're born to win, that you're born to rule over your mind and govern your mind. When you do that, when you digest and exalt it in your mind, it will generate vitality and energy all over your body. That's the blood that you're eating, the body, and you're drinking the blood because you're vitalizing your whole being. You're pouring life and love into that idea. It's a living part of you, and you're empowered from on high.

Do not look for flattery from others. Do not look to others for promotion or aggrandizement. Turn within and realize that you promote yourself, that success is yours, harmony is yours, right action is yours, beauty is yours. When you establish the mental equivalent in your mind, there's no person, place, or thing, or any power in the world which can prevent you from promotion, recognition, or achieving your goal. You're a spiritual being, one with the infinite, and the infinite cannot fail.

You don't want dominion over other people. You want dominion over your own thoughts, feelings, actions, and reactions, and you want that now.

Three Steps
to Success

uccess means successful living, a long period of peace, joy, and happiness on this plane. There is no success without peace of mind. If you have ulcers and high blood pressure, that's certainly not successful living. That's failure.

The eternal experience of harmony, health, peace, and wholeness is the everlasting life spoken of in the Bible. The real things of life such as peace, harmony, integrity, security, and happiness are intangible. They come from the world within. The outside world will not give them to you, they come from the deep self of man.

Meditating on these qualities builds these treasures of Heaven in your subconscious mind. It is where moth and rust do not consume, where thieves do not break through and steal.

There are steps to success. The first step is to find out the thing you love to do, and do it. Now that's simple. Success is in loving your work. If you don't love your work, you're certainly a failure. You're not a success.

Though if a man is a psychiatrist, it is not adequate for him to get a diploma and place it on the wall. He must keep up with the times, attend conventions, continue studying the mind and its workings. The successful psychiatrist visits clinics, reads the latest scientific articles. In other words, he's involved in the most advanced methods of alleviating human suffering. The successful psychiatrist or doctor must have the interests of his patients at heart. If he doesn't, he's really a failure.

Someone may say, "How can I put the first step into operation? I don't know what I should do." In such a case, pray for guidance as follows. It's very simple:

"The infinite intelligence of my subconscious mind reveals to me my true place in life where I am doing what I love to do, divinely happy and divinely prospered."

Repeat this prayer quietly, positively, and lovingly to your deeper mind. As you persist with faith and confidence, the answer will come to you as a feeling, a hunch, or a tendency in a certain direction.

A boy in college is studying philosophy. All of a sudden he stops and he changes over to medicine or something else, because he has asked for guidance to his true place in life. It will come to you clearly and in peace as an inner silent awareness, an inner silent knowing of the soul, whereby you know that you know.

The second step to success is to specialize in some particular branch of work, and then know more about it than anyone else. For example, if a young man chooses chemistry as his profession, he should concentrate on one of the many branches in this field. There's pharmaceutical chemistry, analytical chemistry, biochemistry, and so on. Then he should give all of his time and attention to his chosen specialty.

He should become sufficiently enthusiastic to try to know all there is available about his field. If possible, he should know more than anyone else in that particular field because he's specializing. The young man should become ardently interested in his work and should desire to serve mankind.

"He that is greatest among you, let him become your servant." There is a great contrast in this attitude of mind in comparison to that of the man who only wants to make a living or just get by. Getting by is not true success; that's mediocrity. Man's motive must be greater, nobler, and more altruistic. He must serve others, thereby casting his bread upon the waters of his mind.

The third step is the most important one of all. You must be sure that the thing you want to do does not positively affect your success only. Your desire must not be selfish, it must benefit humanity. The path of a complete circuit must be formed, like a circle. In other words, your idea must go forth with the purpose of blessing or serving the world. It will then come back to you pressed down, shaken together, and running over. It might be a book you write, which will lift up mankind. It might be some great music. You might have some idea like Edison that will light up the world.

If it is to benefit yourself exclusively, the complete circuit is not formed, and you may experience a short circuit in your life which may consist of limitation or sickness.

Some people may say, "Oh, yes, but Mr. James made a fortune or John Jones made a fortune in selling fraudulent oil stock." A man may seem to succeed for a while, but the money he obtained by fraud will usually take wings and fly away.

When we rob from another, we rob from ourselves because we are in a mood of lack and limitation. This may manifest itself in our body, home life, or affairs. We impoverish ourselves and attract all manner of limitation to us. In his ignorance, man doesn't know he's robbing himself—that's how funny it is.

What we think and feel, we create. We create what we believe. Even though a man may have accumulated a fortune fraudulently, he is not successful. There is no success without peace of mind.

Supposing a man has ulcers of the stomach, high blood pressure, migraine headaches, arthritis, or cancer, and he has a $50 million fortune. Is he successful? That's not being a success, because he's not successful in the art of living.

You're here to live life gloriously. You're here to have peace of mind, love, companionship, right action. You're here to release the imprisoned splendor that is within. You're here to have an inner sense of poise, balance, and equilibrium, equanimity and serenity.

You're here to express more of God every day. What good is man's accumulated wealth if he cannot sleep nights, is sick, or has a guilt complex? Though wealth is not a deterrent to happiness or peace of mind, success or anything else. A man may be worth millions of dollars and be very spiritual, Godlike, and some of them are magnanimous and generous.

Many of the multimillionaires in this country and other parts of the world, they scatter yet they prosper. They're doing incalculable good, spending millions to banish malaria and build hospitals and many other things. They can't count the millions that come back.

Some so-called poor people are very envious and jealous of those who've become successful. They impoverish themselves attracting more lack and limitation.

* * *

I knew a man in London who told me of his exploits. He had been a professional pickpocket and had amassed a large amount of money. He had a summer home in France and lived in a royal fashion in England. His story was that he was in constant dread of being arrested by Scotland Yard.

I was his guest one time in a certain part of London, where he was teaching young boys how to pick pockets. Yes, he had many inner disorders which were undoubtedly caused by his constant fear and deepseated guilt complex.

He knew he was doing wrong. He knew he was poisoning the minds of these young boys. He knew they would subsequently end up in jail in London, but he was full of avarice and greed. He wasn't interested in the boys. He was interested in the money they were stealing, from which he would get a small percentage.

This deep sense of guilt attracted all kinds of trouble to him, and he subsequently surrendered to the police and served a prison sentence. After his release from prison he sought psychological and spiritual counsel and became transformed.

He went to work and became an honest, law-abiding citizen. He was able to help others. He found what he loved to do. He was happy. He became transformed by the renewal of his mind.

A successful person loves his work and expresses himself fully. Success is contingent upon a higher ideal than the mere accumulation of riches. The man of success is the man who possesses great psychological and spiritual understanding.

If you don't have all the money you need to do what you want to do, when you want to do it, you're certainly not a success. You should have all the money you need for your family. If your wife needs a new car, you should be able to go out and buy one. If your son wants to go to Paris to study music, you should be able to send him there.

You would not be a success except you were able to do all the things that you really want to do, when you want to do it. Then you're as rich as Croesus. All you have to realize is that God is the source of your supply, and all your needs are met at every moment in time and point of space. Write that in your subconscious mind and you'll never want all the days of your life.

* * *

Many of the great industrialists today depend upon the correct use of their subconscious mind for their success. Many of the great institutions in this country practice the Golden Rule. There are billion-dollar corporations, and many of you know exactly who they are.

There was an article published years ago about Flagler, an oil magnate. When he was young, he was very poor, and he admitted that the secret of his success was his ability to see a project in its completion. In his case, he closed his eyes and imagined a big oil industry, saw trains running on the tracks, heard whistles blowing, and saw smoke, though he didn't have any money yet, as he told the reporter from *Electrical Experimenter*.

He was a poor boy, but he knew there was oil in those fields, and having seen and felt the fulfillment of his prayer, his subconscious mind brought about its realization. He attracted to himself men with money, engineers, chemists, physicists, oilmen, and all the things that were necessary for the unfolding of his dream.

Just like you put a seed in the ground, it undergoes dissolution, and there's a wisdom within that seed that attracts to it phosphates and sulfur, calcium, enzymes, and all things from the soil. When it comes above the ground by a process of photosynthesis, it extracts from the atmosphere and the rays of the sun everything necessary to bring forth the most complex chemical compounds, beyond the ken of the wisest man. That's the wisdom in the seed.

If you imagine an objective clearly, you will be provided with the necessities in ways you know not of, through the wonderful working power of your subconscious mind. In considering the three steps to success, you must never forget the underlying power of the creative forces of your subconscious mind. This is the energy in back of all steps in any plan of success.

Your thought is creative. Thought fused with feeling becomes a subjective faith or belief, and according to your belief is it done unto you. Many of the greatest men in this country who contributed to its growth landed penniless in New York and Boston and other places. Many couldn't even speak the language.

One of them was a man called Giannini, a peddler. He had a fruit cart, and sold pencils and groceries from door to door. He studied and learned the language, and then became interested in economics. He studied at night and he was able to help farmers by loaning them money. He formed the biggest bank in the world, called the Bank of America.

I suppose that's the reason many people are jealous of him, because he was successful. He rolled up his sleeves. He went to work. He studied at night. He pored over books. He listened to his teachers. Then he did good, as there were many farmers who were going bankrupt, and Giannini loaned them money and preserved their farm.

He gave service, and that bank is the greatest bank in the world today, founded by a penniless immigrant. He had a dream. He had a vision.

Isn't that true of thousands and thousands of men, some of the greatest physicists, scientists, doctors and surgeons? Like the great mathematician, Einstein, and many others. They contributed to the world.

⁕ ⁕ ⁕

Knowledge of a mighty force in you, which is capable of bringing to pass all your desires, gives you confidence and a sense of peace. Whatever your field of action may be, you should learn the laws of your subconscious mind.

Get a book called *The Power of Your Subconscious Mind*. Get another book called *The Infinite Power to Be Rich*. I wrote these two books many years ago. They are translated into many languages, and they're immensely popular. They give you the key to impregnating your subconscious mind with success, with harmony, with peace, with right action, illumination and inspiration.

When you know how to apply the powers of your mind, when you are expressing yourself fully and giving of your talents to others, you are on the sure path to true success. If you are about God's business or any part of it, God by His very nature is for you, so who can be against you?

With this understanding, there is no power in Heaven or on earth to withhold success from you. You're successful when you're successful in your prayer life, your relationship with people in your chosen profession, and your communion with things divine.

A movie actor told me that he'd had very little education, but he had a dream as a boy of becoming a successful movie actor. Out in the field, mowing hay, driving the cows home, or even when milking them, he would constantly imagine he saw his name in big lights at a large theater. Here's a man who didn't know anything at all about the laws of mind, yet he was using the law.

"I kept this up for years," he said, "until finally I ran away from home. I got extra jobs in the motion picture field, and the day finally came when I saw my name in great, big lights, just as I did when I was a boy." Then he added, "I know the power of sustained imagination to bring success."

The Bible puts it this way, *"Call things that be not as though they were, and the unseen become seen. I told you before it came to pass that when it did come to pass, you might believe."*

Here's a boy mowing hay, who imagines his name in lights on a great theater. He's living that role in his mind. It sinks down into his subconscious, becomes an impression. Whatever is impressed in the subconscious must be expressed as form, function, experience, and event. That's the great law of your mind.

Thirty years ago, I knew a young pharmacist who was receiving $40 a week plus commission on sales. That was a very good salary in those days. "After twenty-five years I will get a pension and retire," he said to me.

I said to this young man, "Why don't you own your own store? Get out of this place. Raise your sights. Have a dream for your children. Maybe your son wants to be a doctor. Perhaps your daughter desires to be a great musician. Perhaps she would like to go to Europe to study under the Great Carteau."

His answer was that he had no money, but he soon began to awaken to the fact that whatever he could conceive as true, he could give conception. I explained to him that wealth is a state of consciousness, a state of mind. Health is a state of mind. You have as much vitality as you have appropriated, as much wisdom as you have appropriated, as much peace as you have appropriated, and you have as much wealth as you've established in your subconscious mind, because you must have the mental equivalent of anything you want in this life. A millionaire or a multimillionaire has the exact equivalent of that in his subconscious mind.

The first step toward this man's goal was his awakening to the powers of his subconscious mind, which I briefly elaborated on for his benefit. His second step was his realization that if he could succeed in conveying an idea to his subconscious mind, the latter would somehow bring it to pass.

He began to imagine that he was in his own store; imagination the keyboard to success. The ancient Hebrews called it the workshop of God, because whatever you imagine and feel to be true comes to pass.

He mentally arranged the bottled, dispensed prescriptions and imagined several clerks in the store, waiting on customers. Mentally, he worked in that imaginary store. He visualized a big bank balance as well. Here's a man getting $40 a week, but using his mind constructively.

Like a good actor, he lived the role. "*Act as though I am, and I will be.*" This pharmacist put himself wholeheartedly into the act, living, moving, and acting on the assumption that he owned the store.

The sequel was interesting. He was discharged from his position and found new employment with a large chain store. He became manager and later on, district manager. He saved enough money in four years to provide a down payment on a drugstore of his own. He called it his dream pharmacy.

"It was exactly the store I saw in my imagination," he said. He became a recognized success in his chosen field and was happy doing what he loved to do.

. . .

Some years ago, I gave a lecture to a group of businessmen on the powers of imagination and the subconscious mind. In the lecture, I pointed out how Goethe used his imagination wisely when confronted with difficulties and predicaments.

His biographers point out that he was accustomed to filling many hours quietly holding imaginary conversations. It is well know that his custom was to imagine one of his friends before him in a chair, answering him in the right way. In other words, if he were concerned over any problems, he imagined his friend giving him the right or appropriate answer accompanied with the usual gestures and tonal qualities of the voice, and he made the entire imaginary scene as real and as vivid as possible.

One of the men present at this lecture was a young stockbroker. He proceeded to adopt the technique of Goethe. He began to have mental, imaginary conversations with a multimillionaire banker friend of his who used to congratulate him on his wise and sound judgment and compliment him on his purchase of the right stocks.

He used to imagine these imaginary conversations until he had psychologically fixed them as a form of belief in his mind. That's by repetition, repeating a little movie that you create yourself in your mind over and over again. Doesn't it sink down into your subconscious? Of course it does.

This broker's inner talking and controlled imagination certainly agreed with his aim, which was to make sound investments for his clients. His main purpose in life was to make money for his clients and to see them prosper financially by his wise counsel. He is still using his subconscious mind in his business, and he's a brilliant success in his field of endeavor. In other words, he was using someone else to impregnate his subconscious mind with success, achievement, and victory.

There's a boy working with me, his name is Robbie Wright. He's studying electronics, and he has a very prominent position in DeMolay, the youth organization, and he's sent out to collect money.

He imagines that I am congratulating him on his success at night, before he goes to sleep. He knows by doing this he's impregnating his subconscious mind. He passes examinations with flying colors, he's an effective member of DeMolay, and he's on the way to great things because he knows the laws of mind and the way of the infinite intelligence within him.

He doesn't laugh at it, saying, "What nonsense." He's using it. As he says, "Infinite intelligence leads and guides me in all my studies. I pass all examinations in divine order, through divine love."

Then the deeper mind responds and sometimes shows him the answers, dreams, and visions that enable his success as he sleeps. His intuition is an inner feeling. He opens his textbook and knows all the things he'll being questioned about in the examination. That's a very common experience with students who use their mind, they know the questions before they're asked, sometimes intuitively, and sometimes they see them in dreams and visions.

A boy who was attending high school said to me, "I'm getting very poor grades. My memory is failing. I don't know what's going on." I discovered that the only thing wrong with this boy was his attitude, which was one of indifference and resentment toward some of his teachers and fellow students.

I taught him how to use his subconscious mind and how to succeed in his studies. He began to affirm certain truths several times a day, particularly at night prior to sleep, and also in the morning after awakening. These are the best times to impregnate the subconscious mind. He affirmed as follows:

"I realize that my subconscious mind is a storehouse of memory. It retains everything I read and hear from my teachers. I have a perfect memory, and the infinite intelligence in my subconscious mind constantly reveals to me everything I need to know at all my examinations whether written or oral. I radiate love and goodwill to all my teachers and fellow students. I sincerely wish for them success and all the blessings of life."

This young man is now enjoying a greater freedom than he's ever known. He's at Cal Tech, receiving all As. He constantly imagines the teachers and his mother congratulating him on his success and his studies.

*   *   *

In buying and selling, remember that your conscious mind is a starter, and your subconscious mind is the motor. You must start the motor to enable it to perform its work. Your conscious mind is the dynamo that awakens the power of your subconscious mind.

The first step in conveying your clarified desire, idea, or image to the deeper mind is to relax, immobilize the attention, get still, and be quiet. This quiet, relaxed, and peaceful attitude of mind prevents extraneous matter and false ideas from interfering with mental absorption of your ideal. Furthermore, in the quiet, passive, and receptive attitude of mind, effort is reduced to a minimum.

The second step is to begin to imagine the reality of that which you desire. For example, you may wish to buy a home, and in your relaxed state of mind, affirm as follows:

"The infinite intelligence of my subconscious mind is all-wise. It reveals to me now the ideal home, which is central, ideal, in a lovely environment, meets with all my requirements, and is commensurate with my income. I am now turning this request over to my subconscious mind, and I know it responds according to the nature of my request. I release this request with absolute faith and confidence, in the same way that a farmer deposits a seed in the ground, trusting implicitly in the laws of growth."

There are many ways by which your prayer may be answered. The answer may come through an ad in the paper, through a friend, or you may be guided directly to a particular home which is exactly what you're seeking. The principle knowledge in which you may place your confidence is that the answer always comes, providing you trust the working of your deeper mind.

Be sure you don't deny what you affirm. That's mockery, a sham. It's like pressing up and down in an elevator. You don't anywhere.

Or you may wish to sell a home, land, or any kind of property. In private consultation with real estate brokers, I have told them of the way I sold my own home on Orlando Avenue years ago. Many of them have applied the technique I used with remarkable and speedy results. I placed a sign which read, "For sale by the owner," in the garden in front of my home.

The day after, I said to myself, as I was going to sleep, "Supposing you sold your home, what would you do? 'I would take that sign down and throw it in the garage.'" In my imagination, I took hold of the sign, pulled it up from the ground, placed it on my shoulder, went to the garage and threw it on the floor. I said jokingly to the sign, "I don't need you anymore."

I felt the inner satisfaction of it all, realizing it was finished. The next day, a man gave me a deposit of $1,000 and said to me, "Take down your sign. We will go into escrow right now."

I immediately pulled up the sign and took it to the garage. The outer action conformed to the inner. There's nothing new about this: *"As within, so without. As above, so below. As in Heaven"*—meaning your mind—*"so on earth. So on your body, in your environment."*

All of these are great laws of your deeper mind. The outside mirrors the inside. External action follows internal action. Realize this simple truth in regards to success and achievement in your work and business. Say to yourself and mean it:

"Today is God's day. I choose happiness, success, prosperity, and peace of mind. I'm divinely guided all day long today, and whatever I do will prosper. Whenever my attention wanders away from my thoughts of success, peace and prosperity are my good. I will immediately bring back my thoughts to the contemplation of God and His love, knowing that he careth for me."

By day and by night, you're moving forward and growing, prospering spiritually, mentally, intellectually, socially, and financially. There's no end to your growth. God loves you and cares for you.

The Wonders of Disciplined Imagination

"Imagination is the workshop of God," said the ancient Hebrew mystics. "God imagined himself to be man. God became that which he imagined himself to be."

Imagination is portrayed in the Bible under the name of Joseph, for *Joseph* means imagination. We're talking about disciplined, controlled, directed imagination. To imagine is to conceive something. It's to impress it in your subconscious mind. Whatever is impressed in the subconscious is expressed as form, function, experience, and event.

Disciplined or controlled imagination is one of the primal faculties of man. It has the power to project and include your ideas, giving them visibility on the screen of space. We're told Israel loved Joseph. *Israel* is the spiritually awakened man who knows the power of controlled imagination.

Israel in the Bible means a man who knows the sovereignty of the living spirit within, who recognizes the I Am within him as the Lord God Almighty and uses it in his life. He refuses to give power to any created thing on the face of the earth.

It is called "the son of his old age." *Son* means expression; *old age* infers wisdom and knowledge of the laws of mind. When you become familiar with the power of imagination, you too will call it the son of your old age, for age is not the flight of years. It's the dawn of wisdom. Imagination is the mighty instrument used by scientists, artists, physicists, inventors, architects, and mystics.

When the world said, "It is impossible; it can't be done," the man with imagination said, "It is done." Through your imagination you can penetrate the depths of reality and reveal the secrets of nature.

A great industrialist told me one time how he started in a small store. He said, "I used to dream of a large corporation with branches all over the country." Regularly and systematically, he pictured in his mind a giant headquarters, offices, factories, and stores, knowing that through the alchemy of the mind he could weave the fabric out of which his dreams would be clothed.

He prospered, and began to attract to himself, by the universal law of attraction, the ideas, personnel, friends, money, and everything else needed for the unfoldment of his ideal. Just like a seed that dies in the ground, it bequeaths its energy to another form of itself. By its subjective wisdom, it extracts from the soil everything needed for its unfoldment. When it comes above the ground by a process of photosynthesis, it extracts from the atmosphere and the radiation of the sun all things necessary for its unfoldment.

This man truly exercised and cultivated his imagination, and lived with these mental patterns in his mind until imagination clothed them in form. I particularly liked one comment that he made: "It is just as easy to imagine yourself successful as it is to imagine failure, and it's far more interesting."

•   •   •

"Joseph is a dreamer, and a dreamer of dreams," the Bible says. This means he has visions, images, and ideals in his mind, and knows there is a creative power which responds to his mental pictures. The mental images we hold are developed in feeling. It is wisely said that all our senses are modifications of the one sense— feeling.

Judge Troward, who wrote inimitable textbooks on the laws of mind, said, "Feeling is the law, and the law is the feeling." Feeling is the foundation head of power. We must charge our mental pictures with feeling in order to get results.

We are told, *"Joseph dreamed a dream, and told it to his brethren, and they hated him."* Perhaps you have a dream, an ideal, a plan, or purpose that you would like to accomplish. To hate in the Bible is to reject, to repudiate, disavow, disabuse your mind, to reject that which is false. The thoughts, beliefs, feelings, and opinions in your mind are your brethren which challenge you, belittle your dreams, and say to you, "You can't. It's impossible."

Remember some of those dreams, ideas, new inventions, plays, or plans that you had? Isn't there something in your mind that sometimes says to you, "Who do you think you are? You can't do that. You don't know enough. You haven't the right contacts," and so forth.

Well, you have. The right contact is the God presence within you which gave you the idea, and the same God presence can bring it to pass in divine order, through divine love.

Perhaps other thoughts come into your mind which scoff at your plan or ambition. You then discover there is a quarrel in your mind with your own brethren. Opposition sets in.

The way to handle the opposition in your mind is to detach your attention from sense evidence and the appearance of things, and begin to think clearly and with interest about your goal or objective. When your mind is engaged on your goal or objective, you are using the creative law of mind and it will come to pass.

"*Lo, my sheaf arose, and also stood upright, and behold, your sheaves stood round about and made obeisance to my sheaf.*" Lift your idea or desire up in consciousness. Exalt it. Commit yourself wholeheartedly to it. Praise it. Give your attention, love, and devotion to your ideal, and as you continue to do this, all the fearful thoughts will make obeisance to your exalted state of mind. They will lose their power and disappear from the mind.

Through your faculty to imagine the end result, you have control over any circumstance or condition. If you wish to bring about the realization of any wish, desire, idea, or plan, form a mental picture of fulfillment in your mind. Constantly imagine the reality of your desire. In this way, you will actually compel it into being.

What you imagine as true already exists in the next dimension of mind. If you remain faithful to your ideal, it will one day objectify itself. The master architect within you will project on the screen of visibility what you impress on your mind.

An actor told me one time that at the beginning of his career, he was mediocre. He had small parts, but he then learned the powers of his subconscious mind. Every night he'd play the role of what he wanted to be in his imagination. He practiced it over and over again for 15 minutes every night, exalting the power of the spirit within him. He created a pattern in his subconscious mind, and using the compulsive nature of his subconscious being, he reached the heights in his profession.

He was the imaginer, yes, and he was seeing a movie created in his own mind. He knew the power of the Almighty would back him up, and so it came to pass. *"I go before you to prepare a place for you, and if I go I prepare a place for you, I will come again and receive you into myself, that where I am, there you will be also."* That's in your Bible, telling you the power of disciplined imagination. Your imagination goes before you. It proceeds your experience and manifestation.

A young actress who was very successful told me that every night she runs a mental movie of herself, dramatizing a certain role. She keeps running it and experiencing it in her imagination, over and over again for five or six minutes every night. She places a foundation under her dreams. It's all right to build castles in the air, but be sure you put a foundation under them. That movie she runs has paid dividends.

* * *

Robbie Wright, who handles my radio programs and operates the machine for me, recently won a prize in a dragster race. He said he psyched himself up before the race, imagined himself winning and receiving congratulations from his brother and his friends. He then felt a supreme power controlling him in the race. Something came over him, and a supernormal power responded to the image in his mind of victory.

The man who constantly fails has an image of failure. You can use your imagination two ways, you can use any faculty two ways. The man who is chronically ill and always complaining, or the malingerer in the Army, is the man who was an image of ill health and weakness. Whenever man imagines illness or failure, his subconscious creates accordingly.

It has been discovered that many men who constantly fail have an image of failure in their mind, and the subconscious responds accordingly. Have an image of success. You're born to win, to succeed.

Every alcoholic knows that if he uses only willpower or tries to force himself to give up alcohol, it just drives him further to drink. Mental coercion, force, willpower won't get you anywhere. But when he contemplates sobriety and peace of mind and imagines himself free and back at work doing what he loves to do, knowing that an Almighty power is backing up his mental picture, he frees himself of the habit and he is healed.

Walt Whitman had a marvelous imagination. He said when the mist filled the valleys, he looked upon the mountaintops, and when the mountain in darkness disappeared, he fixed his gaze upon the stars. Imagination can carry you to tremendous heights or carry you to the lowest depths. Go beyond the mist and fog of doubt and fear and anxiety and get a vision of spiritual realities.

A vision is what you're looking at, what you're gazing at, what you're focused upon, what you're giving attention to. That's where you're going to go in life.

If you looked at the top of the mountain and said, "I'm going to go there," you will. But if you say, "I'm old, I might get blisters, it's tiresome," you won't. You'll go to the top of the mountain if that's where your vision is. You'll realize benevolent forces, and the invisible presence within you, will aid you and assist you in the realization of your dream.

In your journey through life, however difficult it may be, remember there's a holy place within you, the sanctuary of God, where you can feel your kinship with the one who forever is, the one alone who lives in the hearts of all men.

Through the power of your imagination, you can release the flower of love and beauty from your heart. All the great paintings and statues are products of inspired imagination. Your imagination pictures the ideal, and it is the ideals which lead mankind onward, upward, and Godward.

Where is that beautiful Madonna depicted? On the screen of space, or on the canvas? Doesn't it exist in the mind of the disciplined artist?

In the Golden Age of Greece, 2,600 years ago, they used the law of mind and imagination. Yes, they knew the power of disciplined, controlled, directed imagination, the workshop of the infinite. For mothers who were pregnant, they surrounded them with beautiful pictures and statuary so the unborn children might receive from each mother's mind pictures of health, beauty, symmetry, order, and proportion. The mothers would gaze on these beautiful statues and the child would be born in the image, and the likeness of beauty and order and symmetry and proportion. Simple, isn't it? All the great truths of life are simple.

There's an old fable, like the parables in your Bible. You've heard it before, I'm sure, about the Persian prince who had a crooked back, who couldn't stand up straight. He engaged a skillful sculptor, requesting him to make a statue of himself true to his likeness in all ways, but he said, "I want you to make the statue so that my back is straight as an arrow. I wish to see myself as I ought to be and as God wants me to be."

The sculptor completed it, and the prince said, "Now, place it in a secret corner in the gardens." Every day, regularly and systematically, two or three times a day, he would come out and meditate on that statue, look upon it longingly with faith and with confidence that some day his back would be straight like that statue. He paid attention to the straight back, yes, and the uplifted head and the beautiful brow.

Weeks went by, and then years, and the people began to say, "Look, the prince's back is no longer crooked. He stands up straight like a nobleman." The prince went out in the garden, and behold it was true. His back was as straight as the statue.

Aren't cripples healed that way? Of course they are. Wonders begin to happen as you imagine you now are what you long to be, and play the role over and over again. You'll become that.

A man knows that in order to receive, he must first conceive or picture his desire, picture the reality of it. I once spoke to a young man in the Army, during the war. He was premed and all that, and he was complaining about the fact that he was drafted, and he couldn't be a doctor. I said, "Picture yourself as a doctor. See the end. You have a diploma from your particular state telling you that you're now a physician and surgeon. Look at it."

I explained to him in five minutes the laws of his mind, and being a medical student, he understood. He had a mind.

He began to do that, the Army sent him to medical college, and today he's a doctor. He saw the end, and so he had the means for fertilization of the end.

. . .

Archaeologists, paleontologists, and others who delve into antiquity tell us that prehistoric man carved pictures on the caves of the food that he wanted, the game, the fish, or the fowl, or the elephant. Why did he do that? He knew instinctively or intuitively that some power would bring these animals into his life so he could eat that which he pictured in his mind.

Primitive, yes, but you see, he knew the laws of mind, and invariably these things happened. The particular animal would come so he could eat.

These are the powers of imagination that are within you, and I would like to tell you something I read the other night. It was by Dr. Carl Simonton, in *Fate Magazine*. It's a marvelous article, fascinating, and a long article. I'll give you a few highlights of it.

Dr. Simonton is a medical doctor, a cancer specialist, and he says that with the aid of relaxation and meditation, even patients considered terminally ill with cancer have recovered if they really wanted to get well.

He said, "I started this process," talking about the mind, "with my first patient. In addition to medical treatment, I explained what my thinking was. I told this patient that through mutual imagery we were going to attempt to affect the cancer. He was sixty-one years old with very extensive throat cancer. He had lost a great deal of weight, could barely swallow his own saliva, and could eat no food. After explaining his disease and the way the radiation worked, I had him relax three times a day, and mentally picture his disease."

That is, if I'm a medical doctor and I show you a picture of a perfect throat, and all the cells are in order, then you're going to picture that in your mind again and again, realizing that there's a defense mechanism within you. It's restoring your throat to that perfect pattern.

He said, "After explaining the disease and the way radiation worked, I had him relax three times a day, mentally picturing the condition, his treatment, and the way his body was interacting with the treatment and the disease, so that he could better understand and cooperate with what was going on. The results were truly amazing."

He talks about mutual imagery, meaning the doctor is seeing a perfect throat, and he's teaching the patient how to see a perfect throat, and he realizes the power is responding.

He said, "When I explained to my colleagues what I was doing, they said to me jokingly, 'Why do you even bother to turn on the machine?' My response was, 'I just don't know enough yet.' That patient is now a year and a half post-treatment with no evidence of cancer in his throat. He also had arthritis, and he used the same basic mental process to eliminate that."

In other words, picturing yourself as whole, doing what you would do ordinarily, what would you do if you were healed?

This same man also had trouble with impotence. He had been impotent for over twenty years and couldn't have a relationship with his wife. It took him ten days of relaxing and mentally picturing the solution in his mind's eye. Picturing the solution in his mind's eye, he was able to resume intercourse with his wife.

Dr. Simonton says, "He now states he's able to have intercourse two or three times a week, so when he called me and told me about resolving his impotence, I had him explain how he did it just in case I should need the techniques later on in my own life."

He also talks about being a doctor at Travis Air Force Base, and he speaks of his first case, an Air Force navigator. He was a nonsmoker who had squamous carcinoma on the roof of his mouth, and one that was larger in the back of his throat. The cancer on the roof of his mouth should have had a cure rate of 20%, and the one in his throat about 5%. Collectively, however, the estimated cure rate would probably be around 5% to 10%, since it definitely worsens the situation to have two cancers arising at the same time.

"I should emphasize that he was an extremely positive patient. He was also very cooperative, and after one week of treatment, the tumor was beginning to shrink. After four weeks of treatment the ulceration had no growth evidence of tumor, and so it was doing essentially the same thing, showing a very dramatic response. It was generally outside my experience to get such dramatic response in two separate tumors in such a short time. After one month, there was one small ulceration healing nicely, and about 10 weeks after treatment, the roof of his mouth was essentially normal in appearance.

"The truly beautiful thing was that the lesion in the throat showed the same response as the one in the mouth, and on routine examination it was impossible to tell where the throat tumor had been. Only three months after he had been taken off flying status, this man had unanimous clearance from the head and neck tumor to go back on flying status and resume his profession."

He goes on and on, Hodgkin's disease, and so forth, on the remarkable results he gets with teaching people how to use their imagination in the role of mind and cancer therapy. With the aid of relaxation and meditation, even patients considered terminally ill of cancer have recovered, but he brings out that they must want to get well. Some people don't. Some people want to be sick.

*   *   *

There are people who misuse their imagination. There's the businessman who's successful and prospering, and he imagines empty shelves and bankruptcy and so on. If he keeps that up, of course, he'll go broke, but at the moment he's prospering.

The thing that he is imagining doesn't exist at all, but he's running a movie in his mind of bankruptcy, empty shelves, no customers, and if you run a movie like that in your mind, it's going to come to pass.

Joseph, we're told—imagination—wears a coat of many colors. Surely you can imagine sickness, you can imagine failure, you can misuse any power, but it's foolishness to do so. A coat in the Bible is a psychological covering. You can wear a coat of fear or faith, or confidence or love or goodwill.

You wear a garment, psychically speaking, if you're swimming. You may wear one, I suppose, if you go to see the president, if you're admitted in to the queen for an audience. Naturally you also wear certain clothes at a banquet, an opera, and so forth.

We're talking about mental garments. These are attitudes of mind, moods, and feelings you entertain. The coat of many colors represents the many facets of the diamond, your capacity to clothe any idea in form. You can imagine anything. You can imagine what is lovely and of good report.

You can imagine your friend who's poor as living in the lap of luxury. You can see his face light up with joy, see his expression change, with a broad smile across his lips. You can hear him tell you what you want to hear. You can see him exactly as you wish to see him, radiant, happy, prosperous, and successful.

Your imagination is the coat of many colors. It can clothe and objectify any idea and desire. You can imagine abundance where there's lack, peace where there's discord, and health where there's sickness. The Bible says, *"His brethren said to him,"*—to Joseph—*"shalt thou indeed reign over us."* Imagination is the first faculty of man, the primal faculty, and takes precedence over all the other powers of your mind.

You have 12 faculties or brethren, but your imagination, when disciplined, enables you to collapse time and space and rise above all limitations. When you keep your imagination busy with noble, Godlike concepts and ideas, you will find it is the most effective of all faculties in your spiritual outlook.

"Out of Egypt have I called my son." *Egypt* is your subjective mind, and Egypt also means misery, or lack and limitation. Joseph is commander of Egypt who tells you that imagination controls the whole conceptive realm. Whatever prison you may be in, you can imagine freedom, can't you? You can imagine yourself back with your loved ones, doing what you love to do.

Whether the prison is of fear or sickness, lack or limitation of any kind, remember that Joseph is the commander and can deliver you. You can imagine your freedom and continue to do so until it's objectified, and then after gestation in darkness, the manifestation comes, and your prayer is answered.

The man who's hurt in the ball field, sprains an ankle or a tendon, goes to the hospital and has rest. Doesn't he imagine himself back in the ball field, kicking the ball again? If he didn't do that, he'd still be in the hospital, he'd never leave. But he says to himself, "I'm only going to be here four or five days or a week," and he's back in the ball field in his imagination. You know very well that's true, and you know very well if he didn't imagine himself back in the ball field, he'd never leave the hospital.

I grant you that there are people who don't want to get well. They rejoice in their misery, they get attention and all that sort of thing. You should want to get well, for God's intention for you is that you express yourself at the highest level, and that you exercise your faculties at the highest degree.

Yet there are a lot of people in this world who do not want a healing. They rejoice in their misery, and they talk about it endlessly. They say, "My rheumatism," and they pat their legs gently. They say "my arthritis" and "my migraine," and so on.

Consider a disciplined, talented architect. He can build a beautiful, modern, twentieth-century city in his mind, complete with super highways, swimming pools, parks, and so forth. He can construct in his mind the most beautiful palace the eye has ever seen. He can see the building in its entirety completely erected before he ever gives his plan to the builders.

Where was the building? It was in his imagination. I explained to you that to imagine is to conceive. Whatever you can conceive, you can give conception. It is to impregnate your subconscious mind with a picture of the idea, of the ideal.

Where is the invention? Where is the new play? Where is that secret invention of yours now? Isn't it in your mind? It is real, with form, shape, and substance, another dimension of mind. Believe you have it now, and you shall receive it.

With your imagination, you can actually hear the invisible voice of your mother, even though she lives 10,000 miles from here. Mentally, spiritually, she's right in front of you because, after all, we're all mental and spiritual beings.

She's there, and she's telling you what you long to hear. What is that? She's telling you about the miracle of God that's happened in her life, how she's vital and alive, bubbling over with enthusiasm. She's telling you what you long to hear, and you love to hear it.

You can see her clearly as well, as vividly as if she were present. This is the wonderful power you possess, you know very well you can do that. You can develop and cultivate this power and become successful and prosperous.

Supposing your mother is sick in the hospital. But you don't picture her in the hospital, as you have a knowledge of truth. You're fastening that state on her. That would be a frightful thing to do, an awfully stupid thing to do. If you know the laws of mind, you'd realize the healing power of God is flowing through your mother.

A divine love is healing her, divine love is guiding her, divine love watches over her, and divine love dissolves everything unlike itself. Divine love is guiding the doctors and nurses that minister to her.

That would be your affirmation, but your affirmation has to agree with your image. Therefore you don't picture her in the hospital. She's right there in front of you, and she's telling you the miracle of God has happened, how wonderful she feels, how she's touched by the Almighty. That's what you want to see.

Then you're really praying, you're really understanding the laws of mind, and you're a good practitioner. But if you affirm one thing and you image another, that's called hypocrisy in the Bible. You get no results because your image has to agree with your affirmation. Nothing could be simpler than that.

Oftentimes, I say that 99 percent of people don't know how to pray. Oh, they're using wonderful prayers, but they're picturing the father, the mother, the son in a jail or in a hospital or sick or something else.

·   ·   ·

Haven't you heard the sales manager say, "I have to let John go because his attitude is wrong?" Change your attitude, it changes everything. The business world knows the importance of right attitude.

Your attitude means your mental reaction to people, circumstances, conditions, objects in space. What is your relationship with your coworkers? Are you friendly with people, with animals, with the universe in general? Do you think the universe is hostile, the world owes you a living? In short, what's your attitude?

Realize in your attitude that God is guiding you. There's right action in your life, and you radiate love, peace, and goodwill to everyone in the world. As you change your attitude, you change your entire universe. All phases of your life magically melt into the image and the likeness of your attitude.

If you imagine, for example, that the other is mean, dishonest, and jealous, notice the emotion you invoked within yourself. Now reverse the situation. Begin to imagine the same girl or boy as honest, sincere, loving, and kind. Notice the reaction it calls forth in you. Are you not therefore master of your attitude? The truth of the whole matter is that it is your real concept of God which determines your whole attitude toward life.

Supposing the teacher says your boy is slow in school. He can't learn very well. Let's assume you're the mother, what do you do? Let's assume also that you know the laws of mind and the way of the spirit.

You sit down in your chair or couch. You relax first, and you mobilize your attention. Relax the body, of course your mind becomes quiet. You can say,

"My feet are relaxed, my abdominal muscles are relaxed. My heart and lungs are relaxed. My spine is relaxed. My neck is relaxed. My hands and arms are relaxed. My brain is relaxed. My eyes are relaxed. My whole being is completely relaxed, from head to foot."

When you are relaxed, your body has to obey you now. When you relax and believe, your prayer is always answered. If you do not relax, you do not get results. Relax and believe. The Almighty power begins to function at that particular moment, and when you relax your body, you're relaxing your mind, and your mind becomes quiet and still.

So what would you do with this little boy? You would imagine your son right in front of you, and Jimmy is telling you, "Mom, you know I'm getting all As. The teacher congratulated me." You would realize the infinite intelligence is resurrected in the boy, the wisdom of God anoints his intellect. He's happy, joyous, and free. God indwells him, walks and talks in him, and you would see a light in his eye. He's telling you what you long to hear as the mother.

He says, "The teacher praised me. I'm doing wonderful in my subjects," and so forth. You would run that movie, you'd keep that up, and you would resurrect the wisdom and the intelligence of God within the boy, which is now dormant. But it's there, and the mother can call it forth.

Isn't that disciplined imagination? The boy will tell you objectively what you heard him tell you subjectively in that passive, psychic, receptive state. We are talking about disciplined, controlled, directed imagination, and we're talking about the laws of mind. These things work.

The modern scientist knows it. Your dominant idea about God is your idea of life, or that God is life. You have the dominant idea or attitude that God is the spiritual power within you, responsive to your thoughts. Therefore since your habitual thinking and imagery is constructive and harmonious, this power is guiding you and prospering you in all your ways.

This dominant attitude will cover everything. You will be looking at the world through the positive, affirmative attitude of mind. Your outlook will be positive, and you will have a joyous expectancy of the best.

Many people have a gloomy, despondent outlook on life. They're sour, cynical, and cantankerous. This is due to the dominant mental attitude which directs their reaction to everything. A person's mood of joy is usually short-lived, if they're constantly singing the blues, even when something wonderful comes into his experience or that of his family.

A young boy, sixteen years of age and going to high school said to me, "I'm getting very poor grades. My memory is failing. I do not know what's the matter." The only thing wrong with him was his attitude. He adopted a new mental attitude by realizing how important his studies were in gaining entrance to college in order to become a lawyer.

He began to pray scientifically, which is one of the quickest ways to change the mentality. In scientific prayer, we deal with the principle which responds to thought. This young man realized there was a spiritual power within him, and it was the only cause and power.

Furthermore, he began to claim that his memory was perfect, that infinite intelligence constantly revealed to him everything he needed to know, at all times, everywhere. He began to radiate love and goodwill to the teachers and fellow students, which is very important.

This young man is now enjoying a greater freedom than he had ever known. He sits still and quiet and imagines the teachers and his mother congratulating him on his marvelous work, his wonderful reports. It is imagining the desired results that have followed this change of attitude toward his studies.

If you imagine you're successful, doing what you love to do, and you keep that up regularly and systematically, and you don't deny which you affirm, you have to succeed. You must succeed because the law of mind backs you up.

We've said previously that all our mental attitudes are conditioned by imagination. We said you could use it two ways, and you can use your thought two ways, too. You can use any force of nature two ways.

You can use nitric acid to burn the body or paint a Madonna on a windowpane. You can use water to drown your child or quench his thirst. There's nothing wrong with water. The wind that blows a ship on the rocks will take you to safety if you learn the laws of navigation.

There's nothing wrong with the laws of chemistry, they're dependable. You can combine chemicals in a wonderful way to bless humanity and to heal people from various diseases, or you can go into the laboratory and, not knowing the laws of attraction, repulsion, or atomic weights, blow the place up.

You can imagine it's going to be a black day today. Business is going to be very poor. It's raining, no customers will come into your store. They have no money. And you will experience the results of your negative imagery.

•   •   •

I have taught real estate people, and I remember one case not so long ago, a woman trying to sell a half-million dollar residence not in Los Angeles, but quite a distance from here. She called me on the phone and said, "You know, people don't have that kind of money today. My husband has passed on. My father who bequeathed, he's passed on, too." She said, "I'm a widow. I'm all alone, and I want to sell this place, but people look at it and they never come back."

I said, "Look, this is what you do, and stop your nonsense. Walk through this mansion of yours. You're showing it to an imaginary buyer. You're showing him the whole place, the garage, and everything else, and he's saying, 'I like it. I'm going to take it,' and he's giving you a check for it.

"All this is in your imagination. You're happy about it, and you're taking the check to the bank. The banker is saying, 'Congratulations, you've sold your place.' All that is in your mind. You're showing him the whole thing, and he's pleased, and he's saying, 'I'll take it.'

"You dramatize that in your mind. You're releasing it because you're selling it in your mind, and if you don't sell it in your mind, you'll never sell it, for all transactions take place in the mind. You can't gain or lose except through the mind."

All transactions take place in the mind; that's ABC. Sometimes it's almost impossible for me to understand the thinking of people because these things are so simple, so utterly simple that a boy of seven can understand it. Now, if you can't teach it to a boy of seven in your own home, you don't know it, because if you know it, you can impart that knowledge to him.

You can't want to sell a home, unless there's someone who wants it in the first place and who has the money to buy it. But if you begin to say to yourself, "Who has a half a million dollars today? Money is tight, and the mortgage rate is high," then you're beaten before you start.

You couldn't want to sell that home except someone wants it, and infinite intelligence knows where that person is. You do the simple thing and think, "Infinite intelligence attracts to me the buyer who wants this home, who appreciates it, who prospers in it, and who has the money." Then you get rid of all these people who don't have a dime, only they want to see the home anyway. You're not in the sightseeing business, and so therefore you decree that only those who have the money can come to see the home.

Now you're showing it, in your imagination. You're showing it to the buyer. He's satisfied. You're showing him everything you would show him or you should show him, and it's sold. That will happen. That's the quickest way in the world to sell it.

*   *   *

One time Judge Troward was walking the streets of London. He imagined he saw a snake in the street, and fear caused him to become semi-paralyzed. What he saw looked like a snake. You know there are no snakes in London, but Troward had the same mental and emotional reaction as if it were a snake.

What are you going to imagine? The Bible tells you, *"Imagine whatsoever things are true, whatsoever things are just, whatsoever things are lovely, whatsoever things are pure, whatsoever things are honest and of good report."* Think on these things and imagine these things.

You imagine your daughter telling you what is lovely and of good report, and your son, too. What do you imagine about life? Is it going to be a happy life for you, or is it going to be a long life of frustration? *"Choose ye this day whom you will serve."*

You mold, fashion, and shape your outer world of experience according to the mental images you habitually dwell upon. Imagine conditions and circumstances in life which dignify, elevate, please, and satisfy. Imagine your husband telling you what you long to hear.

Sit down quietly, close your eyes, and wake up. Rip Van Winkle only slept twenty years. Sit down quietly, mobilize your attention, and relax. If you don't relax, you'll get no results from your prayer. When you relax and believe, your prayer always works.

Relax, let go, and your husband is telling you what you long to hear. He says, "I love you, darling. I think you're wonderful." He's telling you what you long to hear. He's promoted, he's doing what he loves to do.

He's telling you what you long to hear, how much he loves, how much he cares for you, how he's promoted, and how life is wonderful for him, and how happy he is in his new assignment. He's telling you what you long to hear. Hear it, and continue to hear it, and don't deny what you affirmed.

He will then tell you objectively what you heard him tell you subjectively, because you're hearing him tell you what he should tell you according to the Golden Rule and the law of love. Then you can't be wrong, can you?

I receive letters from men all over the country who say, "I want this woman to marry me, but she pays no attention to me. Will you tell me how to pray and get her?" That's not prayer.

I tell them, "I can't imagine any man in the world wanting a woman who doesn't want him, provided the man is in his right mind."

If you're a woman, I can't imagine you wanting a man who doesn't want you. To me, that's insanity. Love is a mutual thing. If you're in love, there's a natural law of reciprocal relationship. There's no confusion. It's like the woman who says, "Oh, I'm madly in love with John Jones."

I say, "Well, how does John Jones treat you? What did he say? Did he propose to you? Did he give you a ring? Did he tell you we're getting married on the 10th of November or something?"

"Oh, no, but he's smiled at me, and he's nice to me." Good heavens. That's why I say so often Rip Van Winkle only slept twenty years.

If you're in love with someone, that person has to be in love with you. We have to love everybody, that is to say, we have to radiate love, peace, and goodwill to them, cordiality, geniality, wish for them all the blessings of life, and if you don't, you're in trouble, and you're in lots of trouble.

We have to love everybody in that sense. We have to wish everybody what we want to wish for ourselves, which means you don't try to coerce the other person, trying to force the other person to love you or marry you or something. That's black magic, and it boomerangs back on yourself. It's crazy—that's the only word for it.

* * *

If you imagine yourself, or if you imagine life, as cold, cruel, hard, and bitter, the struggle and pain are inevitable. You're making life miserable for yourself because that's what you're imagining.

Imagine yourself on the golf course. You are free, relaxed, and full of enthusiasm and energy. Your joy is in overcoming all the difficulties presented by the golf course. The thrill is in surmounting all the obstacles.

Now Imagine yourself going into a funeral parlor. Notice the different emotional response brought forward as you picture yourself in this particular situation. In the funeral chapel, if you know the laws of mind, if you're not living in the Dark Ages. If you're not mesmerized and hypnotized and brainwashed, you can rejoice in the person's new birthday.

You can imagine the loved one surrounded by his or her friends in the midst of indescribable beauty in the next dimension of life. You can imagine God's river of peace flooding the minds and hearts of all those present. You can actually ascend the heavens of your own mind wherever you are—that's the power of imagination. You can lift them all up, because it's a new birthday in God.

In the modern funeral today, there's no body. The daughter or the son says, "Would you have a memorial service for my father or mother where all of us gather together? We'll have a meditation rejoicing in his new birthday in God. That's common sense and it's beautiful to see people awakening to these truths today.

There's no one buried at any place, and if you think someone is buried somewhere, you're identifying with cessation, finality, and limitation. You're building a cemetery in your own mind, and you know the frightful, negative results from that, don't you?

Joseph dreamed another dream and told his brethren, *"Behold, I have dreamed a dream more. Behold the sun and moon, the 11 stars made obeisance to me."*

In ancient symbology, the sun and the moon represent the conscious and subconscious mind. The 11 stars represent the 11 powers in addition to imagination, because you have 12 powers. The 12 disciples are within you. They're not men.

Here again, the inspired writers are telling you the disciplined imagination takes precedence over all other faculties of the mind and control the direction of the conscious and subconscious. Imagination is first and foremost, and it can be scientifically directed.

A teacher relative of mine was examining the round towers of Ireland. I was with him. He said nothing for an hour. He remained passive and receptive, seemingly in a pensive mood. I asked him what he was meditating on.

He pointed out that it's only by dwelling on the great, wonderful ideas of the world that we grow and expand. He contemplated the age of the stones in the tower. Then his imagination took him back to the quarries where stones were first formed. His imagination unclothed the stones, and he saw with the interior eye the structure, the geological formation, the composition of the stone, and reduced it to the formless state.

Finally he imagined the oneness of the stones with all stones and with all life and with the whole world, for there's only one substance. He realized in his divine imagery that it was possible to reconstruct the history of the Irish race from looking at the round tower.

That's absolutely true. It can be done, for there's only one substance, one law, one life, one truth.

In the stones of the round towers, the memory of the race. Why? It's subjective. It's not hard and solid. The stone is alive. There's nothing dead in this universe. That stone that you call inanimate matter is alive.

Through the imaginative faculty, this teacher was able to see the invisible men living in the round towers and hear their voices. The whole place then became alive to him in his imagination. Through this power, he was able to go back in time where there was no round tower there. He began to weave a drama of the place in his mind, from where the stones originated, who brought them, the purpose of the structure, and the history connected with it.

As he said to me, "I'm able to almost feel the touch and hear the sound of steps that vanished thousands of years ago." Where does that novel come from? Where does the poetry come from? Where does the story of man come from?

The subjective mind permeates all things. It is in all things and is the substance from which they are made. The treasure house of eternity is in the very stones comprising a building. There is nothing inanimate. All is life in its varied manifestations.

The sun and moon made obeisance to Joseph, which is disciplined imagination, to add two to multiply. Through your faculty of imagination, you can imagine the invisible secrets of nature revealed to you. You'll find you can plumb the very depths of consciousness, calling things up as though they were, and the unseen becomes seen.

It is out of the imaginative mind of man that all religions are born. Is it not out of the realm of imagination that television, radio, radar, super jets, and all modern inventions came? Your imagination is the treasure house of infinity which releases to you all the precious jewels and music, art, poetry, and inventions.

You can look at some ancient ruin, an old temple or pyramid, and reconstruct the records of the dead past. In the ruins of old churchyards you can see a modern city resurrected in all its beauty and glory. You may be in a prison of want, or behind stone bars, but in your imagination you can find an undreamed of measure of freedom.

I can now see Shakespeare listening to the old stories and myths of the day. I can also imagine him sitting down, listing all these characters in the play in his mind, and then clothing them one by one with hair, skin, muscle, and bone, then animating them and making them so much alive that we think we're reading about ourselves.

Shakespeare's stories are stories about you, like the parables in the Bible. All the characters are within yourself, and all the characters of Shakespeare are within you.

Use your imagination. Go about your Father's business. Your Father's business is to let your wisdom, skill, knowledge, and ability come forth, and bless others as well as yourself. Go about your Father's business as if you were operating a small store, and in your imagination you feel you're operating a larger store, giving a greater measure of service to your fellow creatures. If you're a writer of short stories, it can be about your Father's business.

Create a story in your mind which teaches something about the Golden Rule and the law of love, for faith worketh by love. You can have the faith that moves mountains, but unless you have love, you won't get very far. Love is goodwill, it's cordiality, geniality.

It's goodwill to all men wishing for them all the blessings of life.

Pass the story that you're writing and its characters through your spiritualized and highly artistic mentality. Your article will be fascinating and intensely interesting to your public. The wonderful powers of imagination are within you.

It would be a wonderful idea if all of us from time to time would recast our ideas, check in on our beliefs and opinions. Ask yourself, "Why do I believe this? Where did that opinion come from?" Perhaps many ideas, theories, beliefs, and opinions which you hold are erroneous, accepted by you as true without any investigation whatsoever as to their truth or accuracy.

Archaeologists studying the tombs of ancient Egypt reconstruct ancient ruins through their imaginative perception. The dead past becomes alive and audible once more. Looking at the ancient ruins and hieroglyphics, the anthropologist tells of an age when there was no language. Communication was done by grunts, groans, and signs because there was a time when man did not speak.

The scientists' imagination enabled them to clothe the ancient temples with roofs and surround them with gardens, pools, and fountains. The fossil remains are clothed with eyes, sinew, and muscle, and they again walk and talk. The past becomes the living present. We find in imagination there is no time or space.

Through your imaginative faculty, you can be a companion of the most inspired writers of all ages. *"God shall wipe away all tears from their eyes. There shall be no more death, neither sorrow nor crying. Neither shall there be any more pain for the former things are passed away. Behold, I, the infinite make all things new."*

Realize
Your Desire

esire is the gift of God. Browning said, "'Tis Thou, God, who giveth, 'tis I who receive." Desire pushes man. It is the goal of action. It is behind all progress. Desire for health, happiness, true place, abundance, and security, all these are messengers of the infinite within you saying to you, "Come on up higher. I have need of you."

Desire is behind all progress. It is the push of the life principle within you. It is due to desire that we jump out of the way of an oncoming bus. We do this because we have a basic desire to preserve our life. The farmer plants seed due to his desire to attain food for himself and his family. Man builds airplanes and space-ships due to his desire to collapse time and space and explore the world.

Desire is the push of the infinite telling us of something which, if accepted by us, will make our life fuller and happier. The greater the expected benefit from the desire, the stronger is our desire. Where there is no expected benefit, gain, or advancement accruing, there is no desire. Consequently, no action is found.

Failure to realize our desires to be, to do, and to have over a long period of time result in frustration and unhappiness. You are here to choose happiness, peace, prosperity, and all the blessings of life. Your desire enables you to say, "This is good, therefore I choose it. However, this is negative, so I reject it." All choice implies the perception of something preferable over what is rejected.

The idea which some schools of thought have of annihilating and suppressing desire is disastrous in its consequences. If man succeeded in this, good and evil would be alike to him, for nothing has any power to raise any desire in him. He would become dead to all feeling and to all motive of action.

Your desire means you choose one thing in preference to another, and where desire is extinguished, no such capacity to choose can exist. Troward, author of many mental and spiritual textbooks, points out Indian devotees, who, in pursuance of their resolve to crush out all desire, both for good and evil alike, became attenuated human forms, hopeless wrecks of what were once living men.

Judge Troward points out that extinction of desire means apathy, no feeling, and no action. Desire is the cause of all feeling and all action and is the moving principle of the universe. Desire is the creative power. It must be channeled and directed wisely. Desire in its fulfillment takes place in your own mind.

There are no evil desires in the true sense. For example, if you're poor, you desire wealth. If you're sick, you desire health. Health would be your savior. If you're in prison, freedom would be your savior. If you're dying of thirst in the desert, water would be your savior. You may desire love, companionship, or perhaps true place. The realization of your desire is your savior.

You may misdirect or misinterpret your desire which wells up within you. The man who desires wealth may, in his ignorance, fulfill his desire by killing a banker or robbing a store. This is misdirection of his desire, and he finds himself in jail and charged with murder.

Teach a man that there is an infinite intelligence within him which created the universe and all things therein contained, and it can fulfill all his desires, and he overcomes a sense of opposition and frustration. Man's desire for food is legitimate and normal, but killing someone in order to get a loaf of bread breeds violence, opposition, guilt, and self-destruction.

There is a power within man which will lift him up, set him on the high road to happiness, health, peace of mind, and the realization of his fondest dreams, without depriving any other person of his blessings.

*   *   *

A man who was broke, out of work, and frightfully frustrated came to one of my lectures some time ago and listened to the four steps in prayer. He went home and applied them. He had never heard a lecture on the mind, but he said, "This makes sense."

He made a list of three things he wanted. You might call them material, but they were his needs, and he was entitled to them. The items on the list for this man were true place, an automobile, and all the money he needed. He chose these concrete things to see if his thoughts were things. He wanted to prove to himself that the idea of the thing was the thing itself.

What is an automobile? Isn't it a spiritual idea outside your door? Supposing all the motors in the world were destroyed by some holocaust. Couldn't an engineer draw a new design, and we'd roll them off by the millions? Where do you suppose the automobile is? Isn't it in the mind of the engineer?

Every single thing you look at came out of the invisible mind of man or the invisible mind of the infinite. That's where wealth is, and health, and everything else.

I said in the lecture, "The idea was the reality back of the form." Just like an idea of a book, which I'm writing. Where is it? It's in my own mind.

He established a definite method of working and practiced it conscientiously every day, sticking to it long enough to give it a fair chance. This man knew that you do not learn to swim after one or two attempts. He prayed for true place as follows:

"I know infinite intelligence responds to me. It is now revealing my true talents to me. I am aware of my hidden talents. I am receiving a wonderful income. I know the idea of true place and its manifestation are one in divine mind. I follow the lead which comes into my conscious, reasoning mind. It's impossible for me to miss it. It comes clearly, distinctly, and I recognize it."

Within two weeks from the day his experiment began, he signed a contract for a job in San Francisco. He gave thanks and rejoiced in the law of his own mind. He then went on to the next objective, a new car. He didn't have the money to buy it. He said to me, "I know I have the idea of a car. It is real, and I'm going to remain faithful to it. It must manifest."

He won a car in a raffle contest. He knew the secret of the subconscious, that if he identified himself mentally and emotionally with the idea, the subconscious would bring it to pass. He was very thankful.

His next request was more wealth. Each morning and evening, during his prayer period, he gave thanks for God's riches circulating in his life, claiming that his idea of wealth was fulfilled. He fell in love with a wealthy widow in San Francisco, and she financed his new business.

This man established a definite method of working, claiming each of his desires as already fulfilled. He claimed each one separately, but all at the same time during his morning and evening meditative period. If you pray like the above-mentioned man, and if no improvement at all shows itself within a couple of weeks, scrap that method and adopt a new one.

Remember, there is an answer that is as certain as the rising sun. There's a young DeMolay boy listening to me now as I'm writing this. He decreed that his subconscious mind would reveal to him the perfect plan for going to a DeMolay meeting in Oregon. The way opened up, and he was invited there and all his expenses paid.

Last year he also decreed that infinite intelligence in his subconscious would reveal the perfect plan for a trip to Europe, visiting many countries. The way opened up, and all his expenses were paid by relatives. He knows how to use the deeper mind, yet he is not working. He didn't have a cent in his pocket, but the way opened up, just as it did for this man. The deeper mind responded.

If he had the money, I'm sure he'd go out and buy a car, but he won it in a raffle. What difference does it make how you get it? He didn't steal it. You don't have to steal anything. You could have the qualified capacity within you to go to that limitless storehouse within you. Claim what you want. Feel it, rejoice, and it will come to pass.

Cultivate simplicity and spontaneity, knowing that whatsoever ye shall ask in prayer, believe ye shall receive. Decide now that you can do what you long to do, that you can be what you long to be. No enlightened person today believes that a cruel fate condemns us to sickness, misery, or suffering. That's jungle belief. That's nonsense, stupid beyond words.

The God presence is the infinite life principle within you that always seeks to heal you. Its tendency is to restore you. Its tendency also is to illumine your pathway. There is nothing holding you in mediocrity or ill health, or in a miserable condition but your own thoughts and false belief.

Come out of the prison of fear, want, and loneliness. Cease thinking that God is an old man up in the sky with whiskers. God is the infinite presence, an infinite power, and infinite intelligence within you which watches over you when you're sound asleep and digests your food, and answers you if you say you want to wake up at 2:00 in the morning. It wakes you up, doesn't it?

Realize the infinite healing presence is within you. It can restore you. It is blasphemy to say that God is punishing you. It's gross ignorance. Ignorance is the only sin in this universe, and all punishment, misery, and suffering are the consequence of ignorance.

Your mind and body are one. In the field of psychosomatic medicine, they realize it is impossible to tell where the mind begins and the body ends. Research work today reveals that the hidden, underlying causes of physical maladies lie in the tangled depths of the mind, in frustrated rages, in baffled desires, in jealousies and anxieties.

It is silly to blame an infinite being for troubles we bring on ourselves by our wrong thinking, by our misuse of law. If you use the principle of electricity ignorantly, you'll get into trouble, won't you? You can use water to drown a child, but water isn't evil. You can make an electric mine and blow up people, but electricity isn't evil. You can fry an egg with it. How do you use it?

The principles of life are not evil. It depends how we use them. What's our motivation? You can use the power of your subconscious negatively or constructively.

. . .

A girl said to me that all she desired was wisdom. That is the overall desire of everyone, but our terminology is not the same. When you have wisdom, you're expressing yourself fully, here and now. An automobile is a spiritual idea in front of your door. A ham sandwich when you're hungry is an answer to your prayer and is spiritual also. If you sing well on the stage, it is just as spiritual as a man singing the 23rd Psalm in the choir.

The man who repairs the roof of your house is performing spiritual labor just as well as a minister, a priest, or a rabbi who may be reading a text from the Bible or broadcasting a sermon.

Realize that the spirit and body are one. Cease looking down your nose at material things. Stop once and for all separating the spirit of God from the flesh and blood of the world. They're one and the same.

Someone asked Einstein, "What is matter?" He said, "Spirit or energy reduced to the point of visibility." The ancient Hindus 10,000 years ago said, "Matter is the spirit reduced to the point of visibility." They said spirit and matter are one, that matter is the lowest degree of spirit, and spirit is the highest degree of matter.

Every physical act, no matter how base you may consider, it is the living spirit within you animating material form. You are not degraded or demeaned when you scrub a dirty floor or clean stables. If you're condemning anything in this world, you are demoting and depreciating yourself.

Good and bad are in your own thoughts, and you color everything in the universe by the way you think and feel. Do not criticize, condemn, or despise your body or the world. Your body is the temple of the living God. Paul says you're to glorify God in your body, and the whole wide world is the body of God. The world is the dance of God. The world is the song of God.

Let us have our meditation now. At the center of your being is peace. This is the peace of God. In this stillness, you feel the strength and joy and love of his holy presence. Realize infinite intelligence leads and guides you in all your ways. It's a lamp unto your feet. It's a light upon your path. Ride the white horse, which is the spirit of God moving in the waters of your mind. Take your attention away from the problem, and dwell upon the reality of the fulfilled desire.

See the accomplished fact. Rejoice in it. Always go to the end, and having seen the end, you will the means to the realization of the end.

The Unbelievable Power of Suggestion

Call a child stupid, dumb, ignorant, and he begins to accept it, and his subconscious mind responds accordingly. You can also start a whispering campaign against a politician, spread lies about him, and you will get a lot of people magnifying the lies into hostility, animosity, and vitriolic abuse.

Some time ago, I saw a young lady behind the counter in a department store, and I complimented her. I said, "You're very beautiful, very charming."

She said, "Oh, no, I'm not."

I asked, "What makes you think so?"

"My mother told me that I'm awkward, ungainly, and very plain," she replied. She believed this due to the statements of her mother and was full of bitterness, inner resentment, and a deep inner conflict. The real reason her mother said these things to her was due to jealousy, because she *was* charming and beautiful, and spoke very well. I told her that whatever she attached to "I am," she became. Then I wrote something down for her:

"I'm a child of God, a daughter of the infinite. I'm illumined and inspired. I'm happy, joyous, and free. One with God is a majority, and if God be for me, who on earth can be against me?"

As she began to affirm that, she has changed. She is no longer down on herself, as she exalts God in the midst of her, for God is the living spirit Almighty which created you and the whole universe.

*   *   *

Judge Troward, who wrote inimitable textbooks on the science of the mind, lived in India for thirty years. He said, "Once you admit that there is any power outside yourself, however beneficent you may conceive it to be, you have sown the seed which must sooner or later bear the fruit of fear, which is the entire ruin of life, love, and liberty. We are the life principle itself. The difference is only that between the generic and the specific of the same thing. Let this be the great foundation and never admit for a single instant any thought opposed to this basic truth of being."

That's the greatest thing Troward has ever said. In other words, once you admit there is any power outside yourself, and that power is thought, however beneficent you may conceive it to be, you've sown the seed which must sooner or later bear the fruit of fear, which is the entire ruin of life, love, and liberty.

I repeated that because you should ingest it in your bloodstream. You should write it in your heart, indelibly. You should think about it 1,000, 5,000 times a day. When your thoughts are God's thoughts, God's power is with your thoughts of good. That's the meaning of, *"One with God is a majority, and if God be for you, who on earth can be against you?"*

The suggestions of others have no power to create the things they suggest. The creative movement is in your own thought: *"In the beginning was the Word, the Word was with God, and the Word."*

"Was God," means it was created from an individualistic standpoint, for the only immaterial power you know is thought, and therefore your thought is the power. The thoughts of others have no power except when you accept that thought, and that which you accept becomes the movement of your own thought.

Dr. Paul Tournier, the greatest psychiatrist in Europe, said that doctors should stop making negative suggestions because people look upon them as men of authority. A doctor says, "You're going to be deaf in a year's time," and a year to the day, they'll go deaf. Or if a doctor says, "You'll lose the sight in that eye," you believe it, and of course you will.

He says we must get away from making negative suggestions, even though they seem to be based upon scientific evidence, from the standpoint of medicine.

Many religions are governed by thoughts, or suggestions, the power of suggestion. There was an old preacher who said, "If you drink too much, if you run around with women and you're unfaithful to your wives, when you die you'll go to Hell where there's gnawing and gnashing of teeth."

One old man in the back row had some sense. He said, "Parson, I have no teeth." The old preacher said, "They'll be provided for you."

This shows how these negative suggestions about God, life, and the universe are ridiculous. God is the living spirit Almighty, forever broadcasting great eternal truths. The God presence is within you, and our impulses and urges are always life heard. Man's mind is cluttered up with false beliefs, ideas, and opinions. His mind is opaque to these eternal truths.

Suggestions of fear to a man full of confidence and faith have absolutely no effect. It reinforces his faith and his confidence in the principle of success. He knows the infinite can't fail, and your suggestions of failure simply give him greater confidence in the inner powers within him. Suggestions which affect us are those which find the kindred spirit within us.

Dr. Brunt was head of the religious science movement in South Africa, where I lectured many years ago. She told me about voodoo curses, and I visited this particular mine where 9,000 men were employed, with three men in charge of them. When one of the workers violates a rule, he gets a skull and crossbones by a messenger and is told that the voodoo curse is on him. Sometimes the curse says, "You will die at 6:00," and then this otherwise-perfect specimen of humanity sits down and dies at 6:00. I spoke to a couple of the doctors who were present and they said it's true. They says fear killed him, that these men essentially kill themselves.

There were missionaries cursed by these voodoo doctors as well, because they were taking business away from them. But there's nothing in the subconscious of the missionary that generates fear regarding a voodoo curse, and therefore, they laugh at the curses pronounced upon them. The skull and crossbones sent to them are meaningless objects.

But the natives are brought up in the belief that the voodoo doctor has some great occult power, only because these men give them power. So realize the power is in the movement of your own thought, and no one has the power to hurt you but yourself. Who shall hurt you if you're a follower of that which is good?

"No evil shall befall the just, no plague shall come nigh thy dwelling."

"No good thing shall be withheld from him who walks uprightly in the law."

"One with God is a majority, and if God be for you, who can be against you?"

"I will fear no evil for thou art with me. Thy rod and thy staff, they comfort me."

"I dwell in the secret place of the most high. I abide in the shadow of the Almighty. I will say of the Lord, He is my refuge, my fortress, my God. In Him will I trust. Surely he will cover me with His feathers, and under His wings shall I rest. The truth of God shall be my shield and buckler."

Then you're told,

"You shall not be afraid for the terror by night or the arrow that flieth by day or the pestilence that walketh the darkness. No, for His angels watch over you and bear you up lest you dash your foot against a stone."

Identify yourself with these great eternal truths, and you'll build up an immunity, a divine antibody. You become God-intoxicated, and you walk the earth with the praise of God forever on your lips.

* * *

Dr. Bales, who was a great teacher here in Los Angeles and had studied medicine in London, told a group of us at the New Thought movement that in his last year as an intern, he and other interns would give patients a placebo, a little sugar and milk put in a capsule form and colored. Nothing but sugar and milk, inert.

He would tell the patients, "This is a new drug, a new chemical that will take away all the migraines. It's from Germany, a new research product." They'd come back the next week and say, "Oh, Doctor, that was marvelous medicine. That was wonderful, I need some more of that." Yet it was absolutely nothing in the world but sugar and milk, showing you the power of suggestion.

The suggestion by Dr. Bales released their healing power, and they accepted it, as if they were hypnotized. Realize that under hypnosis a surgeon can operate on you, can take a leg off, or remove a tumor and you feel absolutely nothing. Why? Because when you are hypnotized, the doctor makes a suggestion that you'll feel no pain, and lo and behold you are.

Dr. Elsie McCoy, who was a chief surgical nurse in a Chicago hospital for many years, had these post-operative patients who were crying out at night, full of pain. They wanted morphine.

"Oftentimes, I would take a syringe, and take half a cc or one cc of distilled water," she said, "and I would go to the patient and say, 'Alright, my dear, I'm going to give you half a grain of morphine, subcutaneously.' I would inject the distilled water, they'd go off to sleep for 12 hours, and the pain was taken away."

What happened? They accepted her suggestion. They said, "This is morphine." According to their belief is it done unto them, just the same as if they were hypnotized and told, "You have no pain. You'll feel absolutely nothing." They accept that.

This is the power of your mind, a marvelous power. So begin to think about the tremendous powers within you.

* * *

Dr. David Seabury was a great psychologist who passed on a few years ago. His father was secretary to Dr. Phineas Parkhurst Quimby in 1847. Dr. Seabury was the only one in America who knew Quimby's techniques of healing, and he passed them on to me many years ago.

He told me a very interesting story. As a young man he experimented with a ne'er-do-well up in Paradise, a little town in Northern California. This man had a certain habit where every morning, he'd go to the post office, the coffee shop, and then to the saloon.

Dr. Seabury was going to have some fun with him. They tipped off the postal clerk, saying, "When he comes in, tell him, 'You don't look good. There's yellow pigmentation around your eyes and your face is flushed. Have you seen a doctor? Are you alright? Shouldn't you go to bed?'" Dr. Seabury then told the waitress at the coffee shop and the bartender at the saloon to say the same things.

The man went to the post office and the clerk said, "Have you been to the doctor? You don't look well. How's your blood pressure?" He then went to the coffee shop and the waitress told him something similar. He then got up and went to the saloon and the bartender said, "Your eyes don't look good. Your face is kind of white. Shouldn't you see a doctor?"

Dr. Seabury said the man then went home and became deathly ill. They had to call a doctor, and Seabury had to go in and tell him it was all a joke, yet they had a tough time with him. They did it for fun, but he'd actually made himself sick, though these were just suggestions which he accepted.

Your subconscious mind accepts what is impressed upon it, what you consciously believe. It does not reason things out like your conscious mind. It does not argue with you controversially. Your subconscious mind is like soil which accepts any kind of seed, good or bad.

Your thoughts are active, and thus might be likened unto seeds. Negative, destructive suggestions continue to work in your subconscious mind, and in due time will come forth into utter experience which corresponds with them.

Remember that your subconscious mind does not engage in proving whether your thoughts are good or bad, true or false, but responds according to the nature of your thoughts or suggestions.

For example, if you consciously assume something to be true, even though it may be false, your subconscious mind will accept it as true and proceed to bring about results. These must necessarily follow because you assumed it to be true.

Innumerable experiments by psychologists, psychiatrists, and others on persons in the hypnotic state have shown that the subconscious mind is incapable of making the comparisons necessary for a reasoning process. They have shown repeatedly that your subconscious mind will accept any suggestion, however false, and having once accepted any suggestion, it responds according to the nature of the suggestion given.

To illustrate the amenability of your subconscious mind to suggestion, if a practiced hypnotist suggests to one of his subjects that he is Napoleon Bonaparte, or even a cat or a dog, he will act out the part with inimitable accuracy. Tell him to kneel down, and he will. Tell him to bark like a dog, and he will. Tell him to lap up milk like a cat, and he will. He believes himself to be whatever the operator tells him to be.

You can make the sign of the cross on his chest and say, "Tomorrow at 2:00 you'll come back to this office, and you'll tell us that you're a victim of the stigmata, and the cross will be bleeding." He'll come back at 2:00, and he'll tell you that he has the stigmata, and there will be blood where you made the sign of the cross, according to your suggestion.

That's why, *"The word is my flesh."* Your thought is made manifest. You see it in front of your eyes, his personality becomes changed according to the suggestion you give him.

A skilled hypnotist may suggest to one of his students while in the hypnotic state that his back itches, and he'll try to scratch it. He might tell another that his nose is bleeding and he'll try to stop it. To another that he is a marble statue, and he'll stand perfectly still. To another that he is freezing and the temperature is below zero. His teeth begin to chatter. Give him a glass of water and tell him it's brandy. Tell him he's drunk, and he'll play the role of a drunkard.

Each one will follow out the line of his particular suggestion, totally oblivious to all his surroundings that do not pertain to the idea. These simple illustrations portray clearly the difference between your conscious, reasoning mind and your subconscious mind, which is impersonal, non-selective, and accepts as true whatever your conscious mind believes to be true. Hence the importance of selecting thoughts, ideas, and premises which bless, heal, inspire, and fill your soul with joy.

Your subconscious mind cannot argue controversially. If you give it wrong suggestions, it will accept them as true and will proceed to bring them to pass as conditions, experiences, and events. All things that have happened to you are based upon thoughts impressed on your subconscious mind through belief. Your habitual thinking with your conscious mind establish deep grooves in your subconscious mind.

You must realize that your conscious mind is the watchman at the gate. Its chief function is to protect your subconscious mind from false impressions. You are now aware of one of the basic laws of mind, that your subconscious mind is amenable to suggestion.

Your subconscious mind does not make comparisons or contrasts. Neither does it reason and think things out for itself. Your subconscious mind simply reacts to the impressions given to it by your conscious mind. It does not show a preference for one course of action over another.

The following is a classic example of the tremendous power of suggestion. Suppose you approach a timid-looking passenger on board a ship and say to him something like this: "You look very ill, how pale you are. I feel certain you are going to be seasick. Let me help you to your cabin."

The passenger turns pale. Your suggestion of sea-sickness associates itself with his own fears and fore-bodings. He accepts your aid down to his berth, and there your negative suggestions, which were accepted by him, are realized.

It is true that different people will react in different ways to the same suggestion, because of their sub-conscious conditioning or belief. For example, say you went up to a sailor on the ship and said to him sympa-thetically, "My dear fellow, you're looking ill. Aren't you feeling sick? You look to me as if you're going to be seasick."

According to his temperament, he'd laugh at your joke, express a mild irritation, or treat you with deri-sion. Your suggestion fell on deaf ears in this instance because your suggestion of seasickness was associated in his mind with his own immunity from it. Therefore it called up not fear or worry, but self-confidence and faith.

The dictionary says that a suggestion is the act or instance of putting something into one's mind, the mental process by which the thought or idea sug-gested is entertained, accepted, or put into effect.

You must remember that a suggestion cannot impose something on the subconscious mind against the will of the conscious mind. You have the power to reject any negative suggestions.

In the case of the sailor, he had no fear of sea-sickness, as he had already convinced himself of his immunity. The negative suggestion had absolutely no power to evoke fear, yet the suggestion of seasickness to the other passenger called forth his indwelling fear of sickness. Each of us has his own inner fears, beliefs, and opinions, and these inner assumptions rule and govern our lives.

You could say to that man, "I'm going to roll with the blows, I'm going to have the most wonderful experience on this ship in my life," and you would neutralize it. A suggestion has no power in and of itself unless it is mentally accepted by you. There is no inherent power in a suggestion. The power is in your thought.

●   ○   ●

Every two or three years, I give a series of the lectures at the London Truth Forum in Caxton Hall, London. This is a forum I founded about thirty years ago. Dr. Evelyn Fleet, a distinguished psychologist is the director of that forum. She told me about an article which appeared in the English newspapers on the power of suggestion. A man gave this suggestion to his subconscious mind over a period of two years, saying, "I would give my right arm to see my daughter cured."

It appeared that his daughter had a crippling form of arthritis, together with a so-called incurable form of skin disease. Medical treatment had failed to alleviate the condition, and the father had an intense longing for his daughter's healing. He expressed that desire in the words just quoted.

Dr. Fleet said the newspaper article pointed out that one day the family was out riding when their car collided with another. The father's right arm was torn off at the shoulder and immediately, the daughter's arthritis and skin condition vanished. That's a terrible price to pay for a healing, isn't it?

Your subconscious doesn't understand jokes. It takes you literally, and so you must stop giving it the wrong suggestions. There's nothing good or bad, but thinking makes it so. You must make certain to give your subconscious mind only suggestions which heal, bless, elevate, and inspire you in all your ways.

Stop saying, "I can't be healed. I can't make ends meet." Because your subconscious will see to it that you can't.

A young singer was invited to give an audition. She'd been looking forward to the interview, but on three previous occasions she'd failed miserably due to fear of failure, giving suggestions of failure to her own subconscious. She had a good voice, but she'd say to herself, "Maybe they won't like my singing. I'll try, but I'm full of fear and anxiety and so I'm bound to fail."

Her subconscious mind accepted these negative auto suggestions as a request, and it proceeded to manifest them and bring them into her experience. The cause was an involuntary *auto-suggestion*, silent fear thoughts emotionalized and subjectified.

Your thought is your prayer. If you don't know the workings of your mind, how on earth can you pray?

She overcame it by the following technique: Three times a day she isolated herself in her room. She sat down comfortably in an armchair, relaxed her body, closed her eyes, and she imagined she was as relaxed as a wet leaf on a log. Have you ever seen a wet leaf on a log? Picture it in your mind, and you'll relax.

It stilled her mind and body in a wonderful way. Physical inertia favors mental passivity and renders the mind more receptive to suggestion. She counteracted the fear suggestion by saying to herself, "God is the great singer. God is the great musician within me, the living spirit Almighty. I sing beautifully, majestically, and gloriously. I am poised, serene, confident, and calm."

She repeated this statement slowly, quietly, and with feeling, for five to ten minutes at each sitting, knowing that whatever you attach to *I Am*, you become. She had three such sittings every day, and one immediately prior to sleep.

At the end of the week, she was completely poised and confident. When the invitation to audition came, she gave a remarkable, wonderful performance. The law of your subconscious is compulsive, and she was compelled to give a marvelous audition.

A woman age seventy-five was in the habit of saying to herself, "I'm losing my memory." You can't lose your mind or your memory. Whatever you have ever learned, even in your mother's womb, is recorded faithfully in your subconscious mind. It forgets nothing, it's the storehouse of memory.

What most people need is "forgetorant," to coin a word, because they're remembering the old grudges, the peeves, the lawsuit. They remember their losses of 1929 and 1930, and they're still talking about them. They should forget these things, but they don't.

She reversed it, saying, "My memory from today-on is improving in every way. I shall always remember whatever I need to know at every moment of time and point of space. The impressions received will be clear and more definite. I shall retain them automatically and with ease. Whatever I wish to recall will immediately present itself in the correct form in my mind. I am improving rapidly every day, and very soon my memory will be better than it has ever been before."

At the end of three weeks, her memory was back to normal, and she was delighted. She gave new impressions to her subconscious mind, and whatever you impress in your subconscious mind will be expressed on the screen of space. It will come forth as form, function, and experience and events.

• • •

Some comments on *heterosuggestion*, which means suggestions from another person. The power of suggestion has played a part in the life and thoughts of man, in every period of time and in every country on earth. In much of the world it's the controlling power of religion, such as, "You're a sinner," "The Devil is going to get you," and "When you die, you're going to go to Hell." Things of that nature, and it frightens the life out of people.

There were some clergymen some years ago who said the Lord spoke to them. The Lord told them that Los Angeles was such a bad city that we'd all be taken out into the ocean. A great earthquake would take place, and we'd all be wiped out, and California would be taken into the ocean.

Hundreds or maybe thousands left, went to Mississippi, Arizona, and all over the place and of course the earthquake didn't take place. Don't be a prophet of doom and gloom. Be a prophet of God and good.

Some people asked me about that earthquake, and I said to them, "Can you swim?" They said yes. "Well, then we have no problem," I told them. "You can swim your way to safety." You can see how silly these hypnotic suggestions are, but how diabolical they are when you frighten the life out of a person. They sell their home, give their goods away for practically nothing, and go off in fear.

If you dwell in the secret place of the most high, you abide in the shadow of the Almighty. You'll say of the Lord, He's your refuge and your fortress. My God, in Him will you trust. Place your trust in the God presence.

As Taniguchi of Japan says, "When the earthquake or the flood takes place, the truth student isn't there. He's always protected." Why? Because the truth is your shield and buckler. You'll fear no evil, for God is with you. His rod and His staff, they comfort you. That's prayer isn't it?

Suggestion may be used to discipline and control ourselves, but it can also be used to take control and command over others who don't know the laws of mind. Politicians use it, often negatively. They soak the rich, they appeal to the biases and prejudices of people. You know it's a lot of tommy rot, but they're looking for votes, and people are gullible, brainwashed and mesmerized, because if you're emotionally aroused, you can be manipulated.

It's dangerous to indulge negative emotions because the moment you're on that wavelength you're in trouble. You communicate with all the trouble in Los Angeles, and you can be manipulated because you're highly suggestible. You need to watch yourself.

Of course constructive suggestions are wonderful and magnificent, but from infancy on, the majority of us are given many negative suggestions, and in its negative aspects, suggestion is one of the most destructive of all the response patterns of the mind, resulting in war, misery, suffering, racial, religious prejudices, and disaster.

The dictators, despots, and tyrants of the world know the power of suggestion. Stalin practiced it. Hitler practiced it, appealing to the religious and racial prejudices of people. Then when they were highly aroused emotionally, he planted these suggestions, repeating certain things over and over again. Millions of these people didn't know they were brainwashed or mesmerized.

So having been given many negative suggestions, from infancy on, and not knowing how to thwart them when we were young, we unconsciously accepted them. Here are some of the negative suggestions:

"You can't. You'll never amount to anything. You mustn't. You'll fail. You don't have a chance. You're all wrong. It's no use. It's not what you know but who you know. The world is going to the dogs. What's the use? Nobody cares. It's no use trying so hard. You're too old now. Things are getting worse and worse. Life is an endless grind. Love is for the birds. You just can't win. Pretty soon you'll be bankrupt. Watch out, you'll get the virus. You can't trust a soul."

And you begin to talk like that. These are commands to your subconscious mind, and your life will be a living Hell. You'll be frustrated, neurotic, inhibited. You'll haunt the psychiatrists' offices because you're giving these destructive suggestions to yourself. The impressions made onto you in the past can cause behavior patterns that cause failure in your personal and social life. That is, unless as an adult you use constructive prayer process, which is reconditioning therapy.

Pick up the paper any day and you can read dozens of items that could sow the seeds of futility, fear, worry, anxiety, and impending doom. If accepted by you, these thoughts of fear could cause you to lose the will for life.

Knowing that you can reject all these negative suggestions, by giving your subconscious mind a pattern of prayer, such as reading the Psalms before you go to sleep, you counteract all these destructive ideas.

You don't have to be influenced by destructive heterosuggestions. If you look back, you can easily recall how parents, friends, relatives, teachers, clergymen contributed to a campaign of negative suggestions. Study the things said to you and you will discover much of it was in the form of propaganda. The purpose of much of it was to control you or instill fear into you.

The heterosuggestion process goes on in every home, office, factory, and club. You will find that many of these suggestions are for the purpose of making you think, feel, and act as others want you to, in ways that are to their own advantage.

*   *   *

A relative of mine went to a crystal gazer in India some years ago. He told me that this crystal gazer was believed to have some strange, occult powers, and she could do harm or good to a person. The crystal gazer told him that he had a bad heart and predicted that he would die at the next new moon. He began to tell all members of his family about this prediction, and he arranged his will. This powerful suggestion entered into his subconscious mind because he accepted it completely.

He died as predicted, not knowing that he was the cause of his own death. Postmortem showed there was nothing at all wrong with his heart—he killed himself. I suppose many of us have heard similar stupid, ridiculous, superstitious stories.

Let us look at what happened in the light of our knowledge of the way the subconscious works. Whatever the conscious reasoning mind of man believes, the subconscious mind will accept and act upon it.

My relative was happy, healthy, vigorous, and robust when he went to see the fortune-teller. She gave him a very negative suggestion, which he accepted. He became terrified and constantly dwelt upon the fact that he was going to die at the next new moon. He proceeded to tell everyone about it, and he prepared for the end.

The activity took place in his own mind, and his own thought was the cause. He brought about his own so-called death, or rather destruction of the physical body, by his fear and expectation of the end.

The woman who predicted his death had no more power than the stones and sticks in the field. Her suggestion had no power to create or bring about the end she suggested. If he had known the laws of mind, he would have completely rejected the negative suggestion and said, "My life is God's life. I live forever." He would have neutralized it, and he would have refused to give her words any attention, knowing that in his heart he was governed and controlled by his own thought and feeling.

Like ten arrows aimed at a battleship, her prediction could have been completely neutralized and dissipated without hurting him. The suggestions of others in themselves have absolutely no power whatsoever over you, except the power that you give them through your own thought.

You have to give your mental consent. You have to entertain the thought. Then it becomes *your* thought, and you do the thinking. Remember, you have the capacity to choose, and you can choose whatsoever things are lovely and of good report.

Long before ether or chloroform were discovered, Dr. James Esdaile, a Scotch surgeon, performed over 400 major operations such as amputations, removal of tumors and cancerous growths, and operations on the eye, ear, and throat. All these were conducted under mental anesthesia, suggestions given to men and women in a trance state, without any medical anesthetic. They weren't even known at the time. This shows you the power of your deeper mind.

Dr. Esdaile only had a mortality rate of two or three percent. He taught orderlies to hypnotize people and tell them after the operation they'd have no infection. "Your wound will heal, you'll be wonderful," and so on, and infection was reduced to a minimum. All this was due to the suggestions by Dr. Esdaile to the subconscious mind of his patients, and they responded accordingly. Isn't that a wonderful way to realize the wonderful good you can do with constructive suggestions?

I received a letter recently from a waiter in Honolulu whom I had met on a recent trip there. I have many friends in the Hawaiian Islands, and I have met some Kahunas. A Kahuna is a Hawaiian priest, and there are good and bad ones.

The waiter said someone was practicing black magic against him, that he was cursed, and that everything was going wrong in his life. He mentioned the name of the man who he believed was using voodoo or sorcery against him.

Remember that sorcery, voodoo, Satanism, and all these things are words used to cover the ignorance of people. There's only one power, and when you use that power negatively, you can call it Satanism, voodoo, black magic, sorcery, anything under the sun, but that's all it is.

It's a power, but it's not *the* power. The power is the *I Am*, the God presence within, moving as unity. It's omnipotent, it's supreme. There's nothing to oppose it or thwart it or impede its growth or expansion. That's why one with God is a majority.

I wrote a lengthy explanation pointing out that all the water in the ocean couldn't sink a ship unless it got inside. Likewise, the negative thoughts of others could not enter into his mind unless he opened the door of his mind and gave them entrance.

There are two ends of the stick, you know. There's the universal at one end, and the individual at the other end, and the stick is one piece, so there's no separation. That same power is within you.

I said, "This is indisputable, incontrovertible, and eternal truth. God is all there is. God is absolute truth, boundless love, infinite life, absolute harmony, and infinite joy."

I told him that when his thought is God's thought, God's power is with his thoughts of good, that his thought is creative, and that when he thinks of God's love, peace, harmony, and joy, he's automatically protected and immune to all the toxic effluvia of the mass mind. When he thinks of the eternal verities, it is God thinking through him, and whatever God thinks can only result in divine law and order, Heaven's first law.

I gave him an age-old spiritual prescription, the source of which is lost in antiquity: Sit down quietly two or three times a day and imagine that you're surrounded by a sacred circle of God's light. As you continue to do this, after a day you will actually see a golden circle of healing light around you. This is an emanation of the God presence within you, rendering you impervious to all harm. You're now invulnerable, completely insulated from the fear thoughts and negative suggestions of others.

Make a habit of this and whenever you think of the voodoo practitioner or sorcerer or whomever, simply affirm, "God's love fills my soul. I loose him, I let him go. God's love fills his soul."

If you can't give it, you can't receive it. If you can't hate a person, you can't receive hate. If you can't pour out negative suggestions and wish them failure, you can't receive it. You can't receive anything you can't give. Therefore you're glad to give love, goodwill, peace, harmony, and wish for everyone all the blessings of Heaven.

You can have 1,000 people thinking negatively of you and it will all boomerang back to them because you can't receive it. You can't give it. It's so simple, a child could understand it.

The sequel to this was most interesting. The waiter continued in the above prayer process, and at the end of the week, he read in the paper that this voodoo practitioner had dropped dead in the street, presumably of a heart attack. The explanation to this episode is again very simple: The negative thoughts and implications hurled against him by the voodoo practitioner had no place to go, as he no longer received them.

On the contrary, he poured out benedictions and orisons on his well wishers, *orison* an old word for meditation and prayer. Then the proverbial boomerang took place, where these negative emotions engendered by the voodoo practitioner recoiled with double force back on him, and he actually killed himself.

If you're wishing death for another, you're thinking it, you're feeling it, and you will create it in your own mind and body, and you'll kill yourself. Meanwhile the other person can prosper like the green bay tree. Perhaps he's full of love and goodwill, and therefore can't receive it. Then who gets it? You get it. You get the boomerang, it comes back to you with double force.

Remember that you're the only thinker in your universe, and since your thought is created, what you are thinking about the other, you are creating within yourself. When you send out murderous or evil thoughts to another who has insulated himself by Godlike thoughts and cannot receive the negative vibrations, they'll return to you with double force. This is referred to as the boomerang. That's why the Golden Rule is the great law.

Furthermore, to think or wish evil for another is to kill off harmony, peace, beauty, and joy within yourself. These thoughts generate emotions, and emotions kill or cure. Evil thoughts plus the subconscious emotions generated by them accumulate in your subconscious mind bringing about self-destruction, which can cause a fatal disease.

Or someone else may be the instrument through which you meet your death, for all murder is really self-murder. Then you'll say, "Why did this happen to me?" Or maybe you'll say, "It's the malefic configuration of the stars."

Let me tell you something about these stars. You believe in God who made the stars, you don't believe in the created thing. That's "whoring after strange gods," as your Bible tells you. You're giving power to a created thing instead of the spirit which is omnipotent, supreme, the all-powerful one, the all-wise one.

There were two doctors, identical twins, born one after another. One took up unity and became a profound student of the science of mind, prayer, meditation, and mystic visioning. The other took up numerology and numbers, astrology and malefic configurations in the sky. He didn't know that these things had no inherent power. They only have power if you believe in them. If the mass mind believes in these things, and you accept these things, they'll come to pass. *"According to your belief is it done unto you."*

He was told that Neptune was square in sun, and Saturn was square in other, his natal sign, and so forth. There was loss and lack and limitation. He was in danger of an accident and sickness and what have you.

This man who believed in all these diabolical configurations, his house burned down. Then one of his children took an overdose of a drug and killed himself. He was demoted, he was sued, and he was disciplined by the medical authorities.

Meanwhile the other brother—remember, they're identical twins—prospered, was honored and received in foreign countries and had the most wonderful year of his life, recognition, promotion. That brother believed in prayer, and the other believed in the stars.

If you told an astronomer today that you were born in Pisces, he'd laugh out loud at you. Due to the procession of the equinoxes, it takes approximately 26,000 years for the sun to make its complete transit, and about 2,100 years for each sign.

Therefore in 200 B.C. it was in the first degree of Aries. That is the spring sign, so if you said you were born in Pisces, you were not—you were born in Aquarius. If you said you were born in Aquarius, you were born in Capricorn, and so on. All these signs are within you. They're imaginary.

Believe in the God who made the stars, not the stars themselves. Shakespeare said, "But we ourselves that we are underlings." He was a profound student of the Bible, and all his writings are tinctured and per-meated with scripture.

I was visited by a young woman who was emo-tionally distraught over a prediction of a palmist, that she would have a serious accident on or near her twenty-first birthday. That's sort of hypnotic, like she was hypnotized and the palmist said, "You're going to have an accident." And of course you will, because you have accepted it.

The young woman had accepted the suggestion and consequently she was afraid to travel by auto, train, or plane. She was living in perpetual fear and impressed her subconscious mind with the belief in an accident. Having actuated it with fear, it would have undoubtedly came to pass had she not learned how to neutralize the accepted, negative thought. This is how she neutralized it:

> "Whenever I go by bus, foot, automobile, train, or plane, or whatever means of conveyance I use, I know, believe, and accept the truth that divine loves goes before me, making joyous, glorious, and happy my way. I know that infinite intelligence guides and directs me at all times, that I'm always in the sacred center of God's eternal love. The whole armor of God enfolds me at all times, and all my ways and travels are controlled by God and

God alone. God controls all travel in the heavens above and the earth beneath, making all my journeys the highway for my God."

She affirmed these truths morning, afternoon, and night, knowing these spiritual vibrations would obliterate and expunge from the subconscious mind the negative suggestion, which was charged with fear. She is now twenty-three years of age, and experienced the happiest day of her life on her twenty-first birthday. She got married to a childhood friend, and they're extremely happy.

"Whether there be prophecies, they shall fail; whether they be tongues, they shall cease." Yes, all things whatsoever ye shall ask in prayer, believe and ye shall receive.

It isn't the stars or their position, it isn't the crystal ball. It isn't that you were born under a veil. It isn't because of your genetic code. It's because of the cast of your mind that things happen to you. That's the way you mold your own destiny.

When millions of people believe that if you're born a certain star sign you'll have certain characteristics, it's because of those people's belief. Such as if you're born in Aries you'll always want to get the top and the front of the line by hook or crook, or because you're born in Taurus you're going to be a banker, you love money and possessions, and so on.

Don't you know that all these qualities of God are within you? They're all within you. "It's the belief," as Ernest Holmes said about these things, "not the thing itself."

Just like the Irish believe that they'll hear the wail of the banshee when some relative is going to die. Of course they hear it, but other people don't. You weren't taught that when you were young, so therefore, you don't hear it, but it comes out of their own subconscious mind because of their belief. These people don't hear the wail of banshee.

You can hear it; I've heard it. My brother and my sisters have heard it, too, when we were children. We weren't mesmerized, we were told that's what you'd hear, and so we did. These are the powers of your subconscious mind, marvelous powers. The power that moves the world is within you. You mold and fashion your own destiny.

* * *

The Book of Proverbs says, *"Put away the froward mouth and the perverse tongue."* Jealousy is the green-eyed monster. We poison the banquet, and then we eat the food we poisoned ourselves. The injured lover's hell, Milton called it. When you're jealous or angry or envious, you're in a negative wavelength, and all the surrounding negative vibrations move in upon you.

When you are angry, you are highly suggestible, and your mind can be manipulated. People can take advantage of you. Furthermore, you're at a wavelength of trouble, and you're tuning into lots of trouble here in Los Angeles, angry and full of hostility. These emotional states are highly suggestible.

The religious fanatic is emotionally aroused, too. He doesn't realize that every truth is a half-truth and that you must see two sides of the question.

A man says, "Strawberries give me hives." Well, they do give him hives, but they don't give you hives. If it were law, three and a half billion people would all get hives when they eat strawberries, but they don't. Obviously this poor fellow has a bad relationship with hives.

So it's a foolish thing to say to him, "Look, you don't get hives." He does. He has had that suggested to him, or his mother or somebody else told him. But he can neutralize it by saying, "These strawberries represent God's food. It's the same substance as my own blood. They're simply electrons moving in space, and I eat these strawberries with joy. They're transformed by the creative intelligence and the beauty, order, symmetry, and portion so that in my flesh, in my body, should I see God, beauty, made manifest." Then he would neutralize it, and he could eat the strawberries without any trouble.

Say you're irritated and full of carping criticisms, you're down on people and you're condemning them. Don't you become subjectively involved with that which you dislike and criticize? Don't you know that you're molded in the image and likeness of that which annoys and irritates you? Don't you know that you become what you condemn?

It's the nature of love. It's also the nature of hatred, to mold us into the image and the likeness of that which we contemplate. Furthermore, you're on a wavelength of trouble, and so you're in for lots and lots of trouble. *"So, put away the froward mouth and the perverse tongue."*

Realize divine love goes before you, making straight, joyous, and glorious your way. That's a wonderful thing to do. Keep your eyes straight ahead. *"Turn not to the right, nor to the left,"* the Book of Proverbs says.

"Let thine eye look right on, and let thine eyelids look straight before thee."

"With mine eyes stayed on God, there is no evil on my pathway."

"Thou will keep him in perfect peace whose mind is stayed on thee because he trusteth in thee."

Don't settle down and say, "This is the cross I must bear, I must put up with this." Insist on harmony, health, peace, and abundance. *"God made your rich. Why then are you poor?"*

If you settle down in your mind and say, "Look, I'm through. I'm incurable, it's hopeless. I must put up with this arthritis or this lower-back pain or lameness or whatever it is," then you're through. All the prayers in the world won't help you because you're resigned to it. You've accepted it.

Maintain the desire inside. The will of God for you is a greater measure of life, love, truth, and beauty. The will of God for you is health, a greater measure of peace and joy. *"God made you rich. Why then are you poor?"*

The will of God for you is something transcending your fondest dreams. You know very well if you burn yourself, it reduces the edema. If you cut yourself, it forms thrombin. The tendency of life is to heal. That's God seeking expression through you, saying, "Come on up higher. I have need of you."

It's God seeking a holy receptacle that He might express Himself through higher levels, through you, because you are the focal point of the divine. You're God's son, you're God's daughter. God loves you. You are God made manifest.

God is seeking expression through you. *"I am the Lord that healeth thee. I am the Lord, thy God. I will come and heal thee. I will restore health into thee and heal thee of thy wounds, sayeth the Lord."*

"It is the Lord's hand shortened that he cannot save?" No, you must insist on a healing. You don't get angry. You don't get mad at yourself. You don't become impatient. *"In patience possess ye your soul."* You continue to have the urge for healing. You don't settle down. You say, "There is a solution. There is a way out, and I'll never rest until I get harmony and peace, love and wholeness into my life."

Now remember, don't get violent because then you'll only get worse. You don't go too far to the right or too far to the left—turn not to the right, nor to the left. Don't get all absorbed in the phenomena of the world and judge according to appearances, and don't go too much to the left.

In other words, don't bother with your Ouija board. You're only talking to yourself. Don't you know when you operate the Ouija board, it's your own subconscious talking back to you? If you believe in evil entities, then your subconscious plays the role of an evil entity, and many people go insane. They go completely nuts.

Wake up, for heaven's sake. You're simply talking to yourself—that's all. You don't believe in evil entities. You don't believe in fortune tellers or crystal balls, but you do believe, *"With mine eyes stayed on God there is no evil on my pathway."* That you do believe, that your thought and feeling creates your destiny, and if there be prophecies, they shall fail.

How could you predict failure for a courageous man? How could you predict incurability for a man who believes in the healing power of God? You couldn't do it. He said, *"I am the Lord that healeth thee. All healing is of the most high."*

Stop going to the right and left. Walk the middle road, the royal path of the ancients. Your own consciousness is the path. *"I am the way."*

Every truth is a half truth. You must see two sides to it. God is the only truth. *"I am the way, I am the truth, and I am the life."*

Realize therefore that your own thought and feeling creates your destiny. To believe something is to accept it as true. What you decide to be true with your conscious mind, you will experience with your subconscious mind on the screen of space. That's wonderful.

There's a road, there's a highway, there's a main road. It's the road to holiness. It means *wholeness*, you see. It's the path of freedom, but that path is within you.

When you decide to be true, whatever you decide to be true, in your conscious mind, you will experience with your subconscious mind. Therefore believe that God or infinite intelligence is guiding you. Right action reigns supreme. Divine law and order governs you. Divine peace fills your soul.

Begin to believe in all these things. You don't create these things, but you activate them, make them potent in your life. Your subconscious beliefs dictate control and manipulate all your conscious actions. Begin now to believe, claim, feel, and know that God is guiding you in all your ways. The divine law and order, Heaven's first law, govern all your activities. The divine right action governs you at all times. God is prospering you in all ways, and you're inspired from on high.

As you accept these truths with your conscious mind, your subconscious will bring all these things to pass, and you will discover that all your ways are pleasantness, and all your paths are peace. If you don't do your own thinking and your own praying, the mass mind will move in upon you and do all your thinking for you. It will manipulate you.

Then you've put yourself in prison, the prison of fear and of sickness. Do your own thinking—don't let your mother-in-law do the thinking for you. Don't let the radio generate your emotions for you. Control your own emotions.

You have seen on TV soap shavings fed to a hypnotized person, and he insists he's eating apple pie with ice cream. You've seen it many times. Tell him his left nostril is bleeding, and it will begin to bleed in front of your eyes. Put your finger on his neck, and tell him it's a red-hot poker. You'll see a real blister in front of your eyes.

Then you'll know the word is made flesh, for the word is a thought expressed. You say, "Why didn't my parents tell me that? Why didn't the clergyman tell me that the word is made flesh, that my thought is made manifest, that my thought is creative? Then, I would have some respect for my thought."

When you serve chili peppers to a man and he's convinced he's eating ice cream, and when you put ice cubes on his neck and tell him it's a red-hot poker and he gets a blister, then you know thinking makes it so.

Fallacy of
Old Age

"*Even to your old age I am He, and even to your old hairs I will carry you. I have made, and I will bear. Even will I carry you, will deliver you.*"

The spirit in you, which is the reality of you, which is God, was never born, will never die. Water wets it not, fire burns it not, wind blows it not away.

This is life eternal to know thee, the one true God. The spirit in you was never born, will never die. It never grows old. It's eternal. That's who you really are. Age is not the flight of years; it's the dawn of wisdom. As one man said, we must cease penalizing the old, because the man with gray hairs, sixty-five or seventy or eighty, he has learned a lot. He's been through the mill. His gray hairs must count for something more than gray hairs. He's not selling his gray hairs, you know. He's selling his wisdom, his knowledge, the skill that he's garnered in experience, that he's garnered through the years.

I know some engineers who come to my meetings on Sunday, they are seventy-five and eighty years of age. They're consulting engineers. They contribute their wisdom and understanding to many other engineering concerns in the Valley, and in many other sections, contributing to society. There is nothing wrong with their ideas. They are marvelous ideas.

We've been a country of youth. It has been a wonderful country to be young in. We have idolized youth, but now it's a country where it's going to be wonderful to be old in. The aged are making their way in the world, and a large percentage of people are moving into the age bracket of sixty-five and older. They are in the political movement, and they are letting their needs be known to the people.

Age has to be served. We need maturity. We need gray hairs. Had they listened to General MacArthur, as you know, we wouldn't have been bogged down in Vietnam. He said, "You should never send American boys over there. They'll get bogged down. They don't belong there. Train the natives to fight a war if you have to fight one."

Then we did the incredible, stupid thing. We sent young boys over there with their hands tied behind their backs; to fight a no-win war. I heard an admiral speak on it on TV, and he admitted it. Admiral Sharp said, "It was shocking to send these young boys over there with the orders not to win, for as MacArthur said, there's no substitute for victory."

So, we've been a youthful country, the accent on youth. We have devalued the multiplication of years, but we need what we call old age. We need it in the Army and the Navy, and we need it in government. We need it in science, art, industry. We need it in business. We need experience. We need talents and abilities—certain things you don't get in college.

You get experience that's garnered through the years. To be old was considered to be one of the tragedies of life in many parts of the world. Age was scorned. They'd say, "He's an old fogey. Don't bother listening to him." Therefore, it's about time that we listen to those who have had experience and who have wisdom, which is understanding.

*   *   *

I heard some years ago about a Dr. Stieglitz, who is a geriatrician, a man who specializes in diseases of the aged. He affirmed that the mental age in this country is eight years. Kind of shocking, isn't it? I suppose that's why people go to the movies. They're fit for the eight-year-old boy.

A man who works in advertising told me that they write their copy for the eight- or nine-year-old mentality. Tay Garnett, who used to be a marvelous motion picture director, told me that they make moves for the

12-year-old mind. He said, "That's box office wisdom." He made movies all over the world. He said, "That's the tendency." Kind of shocking, isn't it?

Do you go to the movies, and do you like what you see? They're for the 12-year-old, most of them. That indicates how lopsided, how unbalanced we are. We haven't yet come to the realization that youth and age, the new *and* the old, are necessary. We go into the treasure house and we bring things out new and old.

Some years ago, I called on an old friend in London who was very ill. He said to me, "We are born, grow up, we become old and good for nothing, and that's the end." His mental attitude of futility and worthlessness was the chief reason for his sickness. He was frustrated, weak, and almost lifeless. He felt his advancing years—he was over eighty-two—which gave him no hope. His cry was that he was useless, that no one wanted him. He was looking forward to being old, and after that nothing.

Unfortunately many people have the same attitude as this man. They're afraid of what they term "old age." The end, an extinction, which really means that they are afraid of life. Yet life is endless. Life was never born. God is life. You live forever. This is life eternal, to know thee, the one true God. Life has no beginning or end. Old are the night or day, younger than the babe newborn, brighter than light, darker than dark, beyond all things and creatures, yet fixed in the heart of everyone.

Wisdom teaches that age is not the flight of years. It's the dawn of wisdom. Wisdom is an awareness of the presence and power of God in you, and the response of a supreme intelligence to your conscious thinking and acting.

Spirit in man was never born, can never die. Spirit is God, and God has no beginning or end. Your body is the garment which God wears when he takes the form of man. God limits himself by his belief in being man. The word *humanity* means one appearing as many. That's all it means.

God becomes man by believing himself to be man. We're all garments that God wears as he moves through the illusion of time and space. In order to manifest itself, spirit needs a form or a body. You'll always have a body. You can never be without a body. It's impossible for you to conceive of yourself without a body.

This portrays and foreshadows that you'll always have a body. Yes, you have it now—it's a rare body. You can leave your present body. You can be sent thousands of miles away. It's called extrasensory travel. You can report on what you see and what you hear. It can all be recorded. They're doing that in Russia today. They're using it in espionage and in other forms of detection. This is well known through our research and defense departments. These things were always known to the psychosomatic research departments in England and America.

So spirit needs a body, you now know. Your body is the instrument through which the spirit functions on this plane. The spirit and the body are not separate. Man's body is spirit, or life reduced to the point of his ability. Matter and spirit are not different. They are the same. Spirit is the highest degree of matter; matter is the lowest degree of spirit.

Man will always have a body. When you leave this body, you'll put on a fourth-dimensional body and so on to infinity, for there's no end to the glory which is man.

The whole world is really largely ruled by the young. This is a great mistake. It's foolish to push a man out when he's sixty-five and say, "Look, you're an old man. You don't belong here anymore." Because that's the time he has wisdom and understanding. That's the time he's at greatest benefit to the government, to science, to art, to industry.

There is relative little value placed upon the wisdom that is garnered by experience and years of thinking, experience and practice. It is our misfortune that our counsels are too much from the side of youth and not enough from the side of age, maturity, and wisdom. By youth, I mean anything up to eighty or ninety.

When you reach sixty, seventy, or eighty, your years ought to stand for wisdom and understanding. Today the voices of the ages are lost in the chatter of inexperience. Listen to wisdom. Get wisdom with all their getting, get understanding. Solomon says, *"I'm like a little child. I don't know how to go in or go out. Give me wisdom to rule the people."* God gave him wisdom and understanding, and all other things were added to him.

Life is a progression. The journey is ever onward, upward, and Godward. All formed things in the universe are gradually returning to the formless, and the formless life is forever taking form.

Anything that hath a beginning hath an end. Your body had a beginning and an end, but your body is to infinity. Spirit has no beginning or end. Life has no beginning or end. Mind has no beginning or end. You are mind, and you are spirit. Our body has a beginning. It will again return to the formless primordial substance. We put on a new body, for every end has a beginning.

Old age is not a tragic occurrence. What we call the aging process is change. It is to be welcomed joyfully and gladly as each phase of human life is a step onward on the path which knows no end. Your journey is ever onward, upward, and Godward.

Man has powers which transcend his body. He has senses which transcend his five senses. Scientists today in academic laboratories throughout the world are setting forth positive, indisputable evidence that man can leave his present body and travel thousands of miles and see, hear, touch, and speak to people, even though his physical body is on a couch thousands of miles away.

Man can see, hear, feel, smell, and travel completely independent of his physical organism. Nature leaves no gaps. Nature makes no mistakes. It was intended that we use all these faculties transcendentally of our environment. Man's life is spiritual and eternal. He never grows old, for spirit—our life—cannot grow old.

Life is self-renewing, eternal, indestructible. God is life, and life is the reality of all man. The evidence of the immortality of man is overwhelming. The scientist cannot see with his eye an electron, yet he accepts it as a scientific fact because it is the only reasonable conclusion which coincides with other observed phenomena. We can't see God, for God is spirit or life, however, we know we're alive. Life is.

You do not see love or peace or harmony or joy. You do not see the wind, but you feel the breeze upon your face. We are all here to express life in all its beauty and glory. The Bible says, *"This is life eternal that they might know thee, the only true God."* That's in the Book of John, 17th verse.

The man who thinks or believes that the earthly cycle of birth, adolescence, youth, maturity, and old age is all there is to life is indeed to be pitied. Such a man has no anchor, no hope, no vision. To him, life has no meaning. This type of belief brings frustration, stagnation, cynicism, and a sense of hopelessness, resulting in neurosis and mental aberrations of all kinds.

We have men seventy-five, eighty, and eighty-five years of age, and women, too, who come to my lectures on Sunday morning at the Saddleback Valley Plaza, Cinema 2 on El Toro Road. If you can't play a fast game of tennis or swim as fast as your son, or if your body has slowed down, or you walk with a slow step, remember spirit is always slow thee itself in you.

What men call death is but a journey to a new city in another mansion of our Father's house. Our journey is ever onward, upward, and Godward. We go, as Paul says, from glory to glory, from octave to octave, from strength to strength, from wisdom to wisdom, for there is no end to that journey that knows no end because you're in the presence of infinity. Infinity has no beginning or end, and you are infinite.

You'll always remain young when you think from a spiritual standpoint. There's tremendous effort of people today. They're lifting their faces, doing all sorts of things. I'm not against that, but that's the great illusion. You're denying the sovereignty of the spirit. The spirit never grows old.

When you think of whatsoever things are true, whatsoever things are just, whatsoever things are pure, whatsoever things are honest, whatsoever things are of good rapport, and whatsoever things are lovely, you'll always remain young. For love never grows old, peace never grows old, joy never grows old. Compassion doesn't grow old. Laughter doesn't grow old.

The joy of the Lord is your strength. Kindness doesn't grow old, or wisdom, or understanding. These have no age, and that's where youth is—goodwill. Cordiality, geniality, exudation of goodwill, exuding vibrancy, these have no age.

Many people think if they run and jump and try and keep up with their son running around the block, or climbing a mountain, that's a testament of youthfulness. That's absurd. Exercise, of course, or jogging, these things are all right.

Cosmetics have a place in the life of women, too, but most women don't know how to use cosmetics. They sometimes put it on their teeth. They look hideous. They should learn how to apply makeup or go to some woman who will teach them. There's nothing wrong with powder and things of that nature, but the great law of life is as a man thinketh in his heart, so is he.

Your heart is your subconscious mind, and if you think of others lovely and noble and Godlike—what is pure—and if you think of honesty, integrity, justice, goodwill, the laughter of God, you'll never grow old because these qualities of God don't grow old. That's the great lesson the Bible has to teach, that spirit is a cause, and spirit doesn't grow old.

Therefore you'll move onward and upward. Some men are old at thirty; some men are young at eighty. Look at the arteries of some men of thirty. They're old. They're corroded. They're bitter. They're sarcastic.

You take a woman and a man, eighty and eighty-five. They're full of joy, full of youth, full of laughter. They're creative. They're painting. They're swimming. They're dancing. They're writing books or writing poems. They're doing many creative things. They're sculpting. They're teaching Spanish at age eighty-five and ninety. They're accomplishing things. It's wonderful to behold.

These qualities of God never grow old. It's going to be a wonderful country to be old in. Age has its glory, its beauty, which belongs to it. Love, beauty, laughter, joy, goodwill, wisdom, understanding; inspiration and guidance and ecstasy and rapture. These qualities never grow old. They never die. They're of God.

Emerson says, "We do not count a man's years until he has nothing else to count." Your character, the quality of your mind, your faith and convictions, they're not subject to decay.

We have placed a premium on youth, and we've devalued the multiplication of years. A man might be an eighty- or eighty-five-year-old doctor. He may know more than all the doctors in the hospital because he's garnered wisdom through the years. We should listen to him.

You don't kick a man upstairs when he reaches seventy or seventy-five and say he's an old fogey. He's not an old fogey. He's learned a lot. You should place value upon the wisdom that he's gathered by experience, years of meditation, of dreaming, of experimenting. He didn't get that in college. No one could teach it to him. It came out of the depths of himself like all the great inventions came.

Most men haven't accomplished anything until they are sixty-five or seventy or eighty years of age. Our counsel should be taken not from the side of youth but from the side of age.

We should listen to General Singlaub, but he was kicked out because he began to tell the truth. He's only fifty-eight but he said it's a great mistake to take our troops out of South Korea. He's talking from experience. He's been through the mill, and he knows what it's all about. He has mental acumen and sagacity, but they kicked him out because they think he's an old man who doesn't know what he's talking about. But he does know what he's saying.

So we do not count a man's years until he has nothing else to count. Your character, the quality of your mind, your faith, your convictions, yes, and your laughter are not subject to decay.

* * *

I met a surgeon in England. He was eighty-four. He operated every morning, and visited patients in the afternoon. He wrote articles for the *English Medical Journal* in the evening. He was young at eighty-four, full of life, zeal, enthusiasm, love, and goodwill. He has not surrendered to advancing years. He knows he's immortal.

He said to me, "If I should pass on tomorrow, I would be operating on people in the next dimension of life, not with a surgeon's scalpel, but with mental and spiritual surgery."

John Wesley was very active in expounding his convictions about God and his laws when he was close to ninety years of age. He said, "They come to see me.

They come to see me burn." Well, he was burning up with zeal and enthusiasm of the spirit when he communicated to others.

I once met President Hoover and spent a half an hour chatting with him. He was very active, performing monumental work on behalf of the government at the age of eighty-four. He kept four secretaries busy. He was writing books, he was healthy, happy, vigorous, and full of life and enthusiasm. His mind was clear and decisive. His mental acumen and sagacity was much greater at eighty-four than it was when he was forty.

He said that he found life interesting and fascinating. I read some time ago that he spent all his available time writing about the life of former President Wilson. Hoover was a very religious man, a Quaker, full of faith in God, life, and the universe. He was subjected to a barrage of criticism and condemnation in the years of the Depression, but he weathered the storm and didn't grow old in hatred, resentment, ill will, and bitterness—for that's what old age is. That's why some women and some men are old at thirty, and some are young at ninety.

On the contrary, he went into the silence of his soul, communing with the indwelling God, and found the peace, which is the power at the heart of God.

. . .

Let us talk about the man who was trying to recapture his youth, sometimes running around with the young girl, or trying to keep up with his son in a ballgame, or swimming, or things of that nature, or playing a fast game of tennis. He can't do it. He's taking a wild fling, trying to recapture what he thinks is lost youth. But his job now is to commune with the spirit within, for nature slows down the body so that he might commune with the internal God and become spiritual. He's rejuvenated, revitalized.

I remember a woman who was all excited because her husband in his late forties was running around with a girl who was eighteen. He bought her a beautiful apartment and gave her thousands of dollars, bought her a new car, and all that. She flattered him, and took all the money he gave her.

He didn't have too much more to give, so I said to the wife, "He'll be back," and the girl fell in love with a boy of her own age, and she said, "Thank you for the jewels and the car. Now, you'd better go home to your wife. I've fallen in love with a boy my own age." He learned his lesson.

Stop trying to recapture your youth, forget about it. The spirit in you never grows old. Don't let your outlook be external, concerned with your body.

You can't take up the sports you did when you were a boy. You can't beat that son of yours climbing the mountain. That won't bring back your youth, neither would running around with a young girl bring it back. She's going to laugh at you, and take all the trinkets from you. Just like the old saying, "There is no fool like an old fool."

You should learn more about the spirit now, the spiritual nature, exercise it, live with it. The will and the purpose of life. You're here to grow, you're here to reproduce all that's true with the infinite.

Emerson said, *"There is a man that's true to all that's in you and in me."* You're here to reproduce all the qualities and attributes and potencies of God. That's spiritual maturity, and we need that.

Einstein was asked what time was. "Well," he said, "it's like this. You're sitting with a beautiful girl, chatting with her for about an hour. Then an hour seems like a minute. You sit on a hot stove for thirty seconds, it seems like an hour."

Time is relative. Time is our thought. Time is our feeling. Time is our state of consciousness. Where there are no events, there is no time. Time is a series of events in a unitary wholeness.

Rip Van Winkle went to sleep for twenty years. When he awoke in the morning, he thought it was still twenty years ago. When you're asleep, there is no sense of duration. There's no clock there. No time. No passage of events. We say time flies, meaning we're absorbed. We've minimized our relationship of events.

If you had only one experience in your life, you'd never grow old. It's just the illusion that you gather when a long series of events passes before you, how you relate yourself to them. If there were no events, conditions, circumstances to relate yourself, there would be no time, therefore no age. It is the experience of events which brings the changes in you.

I met a woman who'd been in a prison camp in World War II. Her relatives were all done away with in the camp. She was seventy-five when I talked to her in Beverly Hills. I'd never met a more gracious, kind, sweet woman—a very spiritual-minded woman. She was seventy-five years of age, but she looked forty. She had gone through what you might call the tortures of Hell, been beaten and kicked and spat upon, but she reacted differently.

She prayed for her captors and believed that God would lead her out in divine law and divine order, through divine love. She didn't grow old in bitterness and hatred and cynicism or old scars. These are the things that cause us to grow old, that's the cause of age.

* * *

Life was never born. It will never die. How could you say, "I am old, I am useless, I am unwanted?" Never in eternity could you exhaust the glories and beauties that are within you, for infinity is within you. The God presence is within. There is no end to life since there's no end to God. Maintaining this concept will keep you forever young, keen, alive, alert and full of the light that never grows dim.

Your gray hairs are a great asset to you. You don't have to dye them. Be proud of them. They symbolize wisdom, understanding, and strength of character.

Many clergymen receive all manner of wonderful offers when they're over sixty or seventy or eighty because people believe they know something by that time. One man said to me recently, "The only reason I come to see you is because you have gray hair. I believe you have been through the mill and that you're talking from experience."

Ministers find it very easy to get a good position later in life. A retired clergyman recently informed me that he's been receiving fabulous offers from many sources. He is over eighty. Truth, love, and wisdom have no age.

It is possible for a boy of twelve who studies the laws of mind and the way of the spirit to have a greater knowledge of God than his grandfather who refuses to open his mind to the truths of God. You can't be less tomorrow than you are today, for life grows not backward nor tarries with yesterday.

Don't neglect the spiritual life. Life is forever seeking expression through you. Realize the spirit in you is sovereign. It's free, it's God. It's untrammeled by phenomena. It's the ever-living one, the all-wise one, the all-knowing one. *"I am the Lord, and there is none else. I am the Lord. That is my name. My glory you shall not give to another, neither shall you give my praise."*

So give all power to the indwelling spirit within you. That is your living God. That is the reality of you. That doesn't die. Life can't wish that. That's absurd, a contradiction of the very nature of God, our life. That's causation within you. Nothing to oppose the spirit, nothing to thwart it or vitiate it.

Don't ascribe power to things and people and events. That makes you weak and anemic. That makes you angry over happenings. Don't say, "She's blocking my good," or "He makes me angry," or "He prevents me from getting a job." Other people have no power. The power is the spirit within you.

Many people get crotchety, petulant, cantankerous, irritable, gossipy, inflexible, and fretful. These are signs of old age, and if you're twenty years of age and you're crotchety and cantankerous and irritable, you're old and very old. But when you are kind and gracious and full of the laughter of God, there's a twinkle in your eye. You're full of faith and confidence in the only power there is. Realize God goes before you in majesty and glory and that His light is the light, the light of every man that cometh into the world. Then you're young no matter what your bodily years.

You are only as old as the presence or absence that these characteristics indicate. You find the presence and power of God in people who are twenty, and of course they're young. You find it present in people of eighty, and they are still young.

These qualities of God never grow old. Don't ever quit a job and say, "I'm finished, I'm tired, I'm old." Don't retire. Put new tires under the old chassis, and do new work. It's somewhat different, but you're ever active, ever present. You keep on going. Some men are old at thirty and others are young at eighty or ninety. The mind is the master worker, the architect, the designer, and the sculptor.

George Bernard Shaw was quite active at ninety. The architectural quality of his mind had not relaxed from active duty. I meet men and women who tell me that some employers slam the door in their faces when they say they're over forty. This attitude on the part of those employers is to be considered cold, callous, evil, and completely void of compassion or understanding. The total emphasis seems to be on youth; that is, you must be under thirty-five, which is absurd.

Of course all that is changing now. It has to change. The reasoning behind it is certainly shallow. If the employer would stop and think, he would realize that the man or woman was not selling his age or gray hair. Rather, he was willing to give of his talents, his experience, his wisdom, gathered through years of experience in the marketplace of life.

By means of practice and application, the man's age should be a distinct asset to the organization. His gray hair, if he has any, should stand for greater wisdom, skill, and understanding.

ABOUT THE AUTHOR

Born in 1898 on the southern coast of Ireland, JOSEPH MURPHY grew up in a large, devout Catholic family. Murphy's parents urged him to join the priesthood but as a young seminarian he found religious doctrine and catechism too limiting. Eager to peer more deeply into the internal mechanics of life, Murphy left seminary to dedicate his energies to chemistry, which he studied both before and after his religious training.

In the early 1920s, married yet still searching for his place in the world of career and commerce, Murphy relocated to America to seek employment as a chemist and druggist. After running a pharmacy counter at New York's Algonquin Hotel, Murphy renewed his study of mystical and metaphysical ideas. He read the works of Taoism, Confucianism, Transcendentalism, Buddhism, Scripture—and New Thought. The seeker grew fully enamored of the New Metaphysics sweeping the Western world. The causative power of thought, Murphy came to believe, revealed the authentic meaning of the world's religions, the deeper meaning of psychology, and the eternal laws of life.

In arriving at his matured spiritual outlook, Murphy told an interviewer that he studied in the 1930s with the same teacher who tutored his contemporary New Yorker and friend, mystic Neville Goddard (1905–1972). Murphy said they shared the same teacher: a turbaned man of black-Jewish descent named Abdullah.

In the late-1930s, Murphy began his climb as a minister and writer, soon lecturing on the radio and speaking live on both coasts. He wrote prolifically on the autosuggestive and causative faculties of thought, and reached a worldwide audience in 1963 in *The Power of Your Subconscious Mind*, which went on to sell millions of copies and has remained one of the most enduring books on positive-mind philosophy.

After career spanning dozens of books and thousands of lectures on positive-mind philosophy, Murphy died in 1981 in Laguna Hills, CA

JOSEPH MURPHY
TIMELINE

1898: Joseph Denis Murphy is born on May 20, the fourth of five children (three girls and two boys) to a devout Catholic family on the Southern Coast of Ireland in Ballydehob, County Cork. Murphy's father was headmaster of a local boys high school.

Circa 1914–1915: After being educated locally, Murphy studies chemistry in Dublin. Bowing to his parents' wishes he enrolls briefly in a Jesuit seminary. Dissatisfied with his studies, and unbelieving of the doctrine of no salvation outside the church, Murphy leaves seminary.

Circa 1916–1918: Murphy works as a pharmacist for England's Royal Army Medical Corps during World War I.

1918–1921: Murphy works as a pharmacist in Dublin. He earns a monthly salary of about $10.

1922: Dissatisfied with traditional religion and finding limited opportunities to practice as a chemist, Murphy just shy of age 24 arrives in New York City on April 17,

1922. He is accompanied by his wife, Madolyn, who is eight years his senior (wedding date unknown). He arrives with $23. Applies for citizenship in August.

1923–1938: Murphy works as a pharmacist in New York City including at a pharmacy counter at the Algonquin Hotel. He deepens his study into metaphysics and years later recounts having studied with the figure of Abdullah, a black man of Jewish descent whom Murphy's contemporary and fellow New Yorker, Neville Goddard (1905–1972), wrote that he studied with. Murphy reports that Abdullah tells Murphy that he actually had three brothers, not two. Upon checking with his mother, Murphy discovers that he had a third brother who died at birth and was never spoken of.

Circa 1931: Murphy begins attending the Church of the Healing Christ in New York City, presided over by Emmet Fox.

Circa 1938: Murphy is ordained as a Divine Science minster. He continues to work as a druggist and chemist.

1941: Murphy begins broadcasting metaphysical sermons over the radio.

1942: Murphy enlists as a pharmacist in the New York State National Guard, a post he holds until 1948.

1943: Murphy studies Tarot in New York City and comes to believe in symbolic correspondences between the Tarot cards and Scripture.

1945: Murphy writes his first book, *This Is It: The Art Of Metaphysical Demonstration.*

1946: Murphy is ordained as a Religious Science Minister in Los Angeles. He soon takes over the pulpit of the Institute for Religious Science in Rochester, New York. He publishes the short works *Wheels of Truth, The Perfect Answer,* and *Fear Not.*

1948: Murphy publishes *St. John Speaks, Love is Freedom,* and *The Twelve Powers Mystically Explained.*

1949: Murphy is re-ordained into Divine Science and becomes minister of the Los Angeles Divine Science Church, a post he will hold for the next 28 years. Services become so popular that they are held at the Wilshire Ebell Theater.

1952: Publishes *Riches Are Your Right.*

1953: Publishes *The Miracles of Your Mind, The Fragrance of God,* and *How to Use the Power of Prayer.*

1954: Publishes *The Magic of Faith* and *The Meaning of Reincarnation,* one of his most controversial books.

1955: Publishes *Believe in Yourself* and *How to Attract Money*, one of his most enduringly popular works.

1956: Murphy writes *Traveling With God* in which he recounts his international speaking tours, comparing New Thought with various global traditions. He also publishes *Peace Within Yourself* (*St. John Speaks* revised) and *Prayer Is the Answer*.

1957: Publishes *How to Use Your Healing Power*.

1958: Publishes the short works *Quiet Moments with God, Pray Your Way Through It, The Healing Power of Love, Stay Young Forever, Mental Poisons and Their Antidotes*, and *How to Pray With a Deck of Cards*.

1959: Publishes *Living Without Strain*.

1960: Publishes *Techniques in Prayer Therapy*.

1961: Publishes *You Can Change Your Whole Life* and *Nuclear Religion*.

1962: Publishes *Why Did This Happen to Me?*

1963: Publishes *The Power of Your Subconscious Mind*, which becomes a worldwide bestseller and a landmark of New Thought philosophy. The book's publication makes Murphy into one of the most widely known metaphysical writers in the world.

1964: Publishes *The Miracle of Mind Dynamics*.

1965: Publishes *The Amazing Laws of Cosmic Mind Power*.

1966: Publishes *Your Infinite Power to Be Rich*.

1968: Publishes *The Cosmic Power Within You*.

1969: Publishes *Infinite Power for Richer Living*.

1970: Publishes *Secrets of the I Ching*.

1971: Publishes *Psychic Perception: The Magic of Extra-sensory Perception*.

1972: Publishes *Miracle Power for Infinite Riches*

1973: Publishes *Telepsychics: The Magic Power of Perfect Living*.

1974: Publishes *The Cosmic Energizer: Miracle Power of the Universe*.

1976: Murphy's first wife Madolyn dies. He marries his secretary, Jean L. Murphy (nee Wright), also a Divine Science minister. He writes *Great Bible Truths for Human Problems*.

1977: Publishes *Within You Is the Power*

1979: Publishes *Songs of God*

1980: Publishes *How to Use the Laws of Mind*

1981: Murphy dies on December 16 in Laguna Hills, CA, where he and his wife Jean are living at the Leisure World retirement community, now known as Laguna Woods Village.

1982: *These Truths Can Change Your Life* is published posthumously.

1987: Canadian writer Bernard Cantin publishes the French language work *Joseph Murphy se raconte à Bernard Cantin* [*Joseph Murphy Speaks to Bernard Cantin*] with Quebec's Éditions Un Monde Différent. The book is based on an extended series of interviews Cantin conducted with Murphy before his death and provides a rare window into Murphy's career. It does not appear in English. *The Collected Essays of Joseph Murphy* is published posthumously.

9 781722 505561